6- 4/13

An Altar in the World

An Altar in the World

A GEOGRAPHY OF FAITH

Barbara Brown Taylor

HarperOne
An Imprint of HarperCollinsPublishers

HarperOne

Biblical quotations are from NRSV unless otherwise noted.

FIRST EDITION

Designed by Level C

Library of Congress Cataloging-in-Publication Data

Taylor, Barbara Brown.
An altar in the world : a geography of faith / Barbara Brown Taylor. — 1st ed.
p. cm.
ISBN 978-0-06-137046-5
1. Taylor, Barbara Brown. 2. Episcopal Church—Clergy—Biography.
3. Anglican Communion—United States—Clergy—Biography.
4. Spiritual life—Christianity. I. Title.
BX5995.T26A3   2009
283.092—dc22   2009018303

09 10 11 12 13 QF 10 9 8 7 6 5 4 3 2 1

For Claire and Kathleen

And when you turn to the right or when you turn to the left, your ears shall hear a word behind you, saying, "This is the way; walk in it."

—Isaiah 30:21

Seek not to follow in the footsteps of the men of old; rather, seek what they sought.

—Gautama Buddha

The whole way to heaven is heaven itself.

—Teresa of Avila

Contents

Introduction   xiii

1 The Practice of Waking Up to God   1
   Vision

2 The Practice of Paying Attention   17
   Reverence

3 The Practice of Wearing Skin   35
   Incarnation

4 The Practice of Walking on the Earth   53
   Groundedness

5 The Practice of Getting Lost   69
   Wilderness

6 The Practice of Encountering Others   87
   Community

7 The Practice of Living with Purpose   107
   Vocation

8 The Practice of Saying No   121
   Sabbath

9 The Practice of Carrying Water   141
   Physical Labor

10 The Practice of Feeling Pain   155
   Breakthrough

11 The Practice of Being Present to God   175
   Prayer

12 The Practice of Pronouncing Blessings   193
   Benediction

   Acknowledgments   211

   Notes   213

   Permissions   217

The tender flesh itself
   will be found one day
—quite surprisingly—
   to be capable of receiving,
and yes, full
   capable of embracing
the searing energies of God.
   Go figure. Fear not.
For even at its beginning
   the humble clay received
God's art, whereby
   one part became the eye,
another the ear, and yet
   another this impetuous hand.
Therefore, the flesh
   is not to be excluded
from the wisdom and the power
   that now and ever animates
all things. His life-giving
   agency is made perfect,
we are told, in weakness—
   made perfect in the flesh.
      —St. Irenaeus (c. 125–c. 210),
        adapted and translated
         by Scott Cairns[1]

Introduction

If I had a dollar for every time I heard someone say, "I am spiritual but not religious," then I might not be any wiser about what that means—but I would be richer. I hear the phrase on the radio. I read it in interviews. People often say it to my face when they learn that I am a religion professor who spent years as a parish priest.

In that context, people are usually trying to tell me that they have a sense of the divine depths of things but they are not churchgoers. They want to grow closer to God, but not at the cost of creeds, confessions, and religious wars large or small. Some of them have resigned from religions they once belonged to, taking what was helpful with them while leaving the rest behind. Others have collected wisdom from the four corners of the world, which they use like cooks with a pantry full of spices. Plenty of them are satisfied, too, even as they confess that they are sometimes lonely.

I think I know what they mean by "religious." It is the "spiritual" part that is harder to grasp. My guess is they do not use that word in reference to a formal set of beliefs, since that belongs on the religion side of the page. It may be the name for a longing— for more meaning, more feeling, more connection, more life. When I hear people talk about spirituality, that seems to be what they are describing. They know there is more to life than what meets the eye. They have drawn close to this "More" in nature, in love, in art, in grief. They would be happy for someone to teach them how to spend more time in the presence of this deeper reality, but when they visit the places where such knowledge is supposed to be found, they often find the rituals hollow and the language antique.

Even religious people are vulnerable to this longing. Those who belong to communities of faith have acquired a certain patience with what is sometimes called organized religion. They have learned to forgive its shortcomings as they have learned to forgive themselves. They do not expect their institutions to stand in for God, and they are happy to use inherited maps for some of life's journeys. They do not need to walk off every cliff all by themselves. Yet they too can harbor the sense that there is more to life than they are being shown. Where is the secret hidden? Who has the key to the treasure box of More?

People seem willing to look all over the place for this treasure. They will spend hours launching prayers into the heavens. They will travel halfway around the world to visit a monastery in India or to take part in a mission trip to Belize. The last place most people look is right under their feet, in the everyday activities, accidents, and encounters of their lives. What possible spiritual significance could a trip to the grocery store have? How could something as common as a toothache be a door to greater life?

No one longs for what he or she already has, and yet the accumulated insight of those wise about the spiritual life suggests that the reason so many of us cannot see the red X that marks the spot is because we are standing on it. The treasure we seek requires no lengthy expedition, no expensive equipment, no superior aptitude or special company. All we lack is the willingness to imagine that we already have everything we need. The only thing missing is our consent to be where we are.

Many years ago now, a wise old priest invited me to come speak at his church in Alabama. "What do you want me to talk about?" I asked him.

"Come tell us what is saving your life now," he answered. It was as if he had swept his arm across a dusty table and brushed all the formal china to the ground. I did not have to try to say correct things that were true for everyone. I did not have to use theological language that conformed to the historical teachings of the church. All I had to do was figure out what my life depended on. All I had to do was figure out how I stayed as close to that reality as I could, and then find some way to talk about it that helped my listeners figure out those same things for themselves.

The answers I gave all those years ago are not the same answers I would give today—that is the beauty of the question—but the principle is the same. What is saving my life now is the conviction that there is no spiritual treasure to be found apart from the bodily experiences of human life on earth. My life depends on engaging the most ordinary physical activities with the most exquisite attention I can give them. My life depends on ignoring all touted distinctions between the secular and the sacred, the physical and the spiritual, the body and the soul. What is saving my life now is becoming more fully human, trusting that there is no way to God apart from real life in the real world.

Every chapter in this book is a tentative answer to the question that priest asked me so many years ago. For want of a better word, each focuses on a certain *practice*—a certain exercise in being human that requires a body as well as a soul. Each helps me live with my longing for More. Each trusts that *doing* something is at least as valuable as reading books about it, thinking about it, or sitting around talking about it. Who wants to study a menu when you can eat a meal? The chapters do not build on one another in any methodical way. They do not bank on literal truth or promise visible results. Instead, they trust the practices to deliver the wisdom each practitioner needs to know. They trust the body to enlighten the soul.

In a world of too much information about almost everything, bodily practices can provide great relief. To make bread or love, to dig in the earth, to feed an animal or cook for a stranger—these activities require no extensive commentary, no lucid theology. All they require is someone willing to bend, reach, chop, stir. Most of these tasks are so full of pleasure that there is no need to complicate things by calling them holy. And yet these are the same activities that change lives, sometimes all at once and sometimes more slowly, the way dripping water changes stone. In a world where faith is often construed as a way of thinking, bodily practices remind the willing that faith is a way of life.

SOME OF THE PRACTICES that follow—walking meditation, pilgrimage, fasting, and prayer—have long histories in the religions of the world. Others are so ordinary that their names do not even give them away: eating, singing, bathing, and giving birth. Religion could never have survived without such practices. Even now, purposeful return to these practices has the power to save religions that have just about run out of breath.

If you have run out of breath yourself—or out of faith—then this book is for you. Since it is a field guide and not a curriculum, you may start where you like and end where you like. I have no idea what you will see when you look at your life—but if you are tired of arguing about religion, tired of reading about spirituality, tired of talk-talk-talking about things that matter without doing a single thing that matters yourself, then the pages that follow are dedicated to you. My hope is that reading them will help you see the red X under your feet. To put it another way, my hope is that reading them will help you recognize some of the altars in this world—ordinary-looking places where human beings have met and may continue to meet up with the divine More that they sometimes call God.

Like anyone else, I am limited by my experience. The practices in this book grow from that experience in all its particularity, including my long immersion in the practices of Christian faith. I trust that those practices, like the central practices of all the world's great faiths, are meant to teach people what it means to be more fully human. Without that confidence, I could not offer them to you. Whoever you are, you are human. Wherever you are, you live in the world, which is just waiting for you to notice the holiness in it. So welcome to your own priesthood, practiced at the altar of your own life. The good news is that you have everything you need to begin.

Barbara Brown Taylor
Easter Season 2008

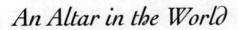

An Altar in the World

1

The Practice of Waking Up to God

VISION

The day of my spiritual awakening was the day I saw—
and knew I saw—all things in God and God in all things.
                                                    —*Mechtild of Magdeburg*

M any years ago now I went for a long walk on the big island
of Hawaii, using an old trail that runs along the lava cliffs
at the edge of the sea. More than once the waves drenched me,
slamming into the cliffs and shooting twenty feet into the air.
More than once I saw double rainbows in the drops that fell back
into the sea. The island had already won my heart. Part of it was
the sheer gorgeousness of the place, but the ground also felt different under my feet. I was aware of how young it was: the newest
earth on the face of the earth, with a nearby volcano still making
new earth even as I walked. In my experience, every place has its
own spirit, its own character and depth. If I had grown up in the

Arizona desert, I would be a different person than the one who grew up in a leafy suburb of Atlanta. If I lived by the ocean even now, my senses would be tuned to an entirely different key than the one I use in the foothills of the Appalachians.

On the big island of Hawaii, I could feel the adolescent energy of the lava rock under my feet. The spirit of that land was ebullient, unrefined, entirely pleased with itself. Its divinity had not yet suffered from the imposition of shopping malls, beach homes, or luxury hotels. I caught its youthfulness and walked farther that day than I thought I could, ending up at a small tidal pool on the far southwestern tip of the island.

After the crashing of the waves, the sanctuary of the still pool hit me with the sound of sheer silence. The calm water lay so green and cool before me that it calmed me too. Nothing stirred the face of the water save the breeze coming off the ocean, which caused it to wrinkle from time to time. Walking around the pool, I came to three stones set upright near the edge where the water was deepest. All three were shaped like fat baguettes, with the tallest one in the middle. The other two were set snug up against it, the same grey color as humpbacked whales. All together, they announced that something significant had happened in that place. I was not the first person to be affected by it. Whoever had come before me had set up an altar, and though I might never know what that person had encountered there, I knew the name of the place: Bethel, House of God.

At least that is what Jacob called the place where he encountered God—not on a gorgeous island but in a rocky wilderness—where he saw something that changed his life forever. The first time I read Jacob's story in the Bible, I knew it was true whether it ever happened or not. There he was, still a young man, running away from home because his whole screwy family had finally imploded. His father was dying. He and his twin brother, Esau, had both wanted their father's blessing. Jacob's mother had colluded with him to get it, and though his scheme worked, it enraged his brother to the point that Jacob fled for his life. He and his brother were not identical twins. Esau could have squashed him like a bug. So Jacob left with little more than the clothes on his back, and when he had walked as far as he could, he looked around for a stone he could use for a pillow.

When he had found one the right size, Jacob lay down to sleep, turning his cheek against the stone that was still warm from the sun. Maybe the dream was in the stone, or maybe it fell out of the sky. Wherever the dream came from, it was vivid: a ladder set up on the earth, with the top of it reaching to heaven and the angels of God ascending and descending it like bright-winged ants. Then, all of a sudden, God was there beside Jacob, without a single trumpet for warning, promising him safety, children, land. "Remember, I am with you," God said to him. "I will not leave you until I have done what I have promised you."

Jacob woke while God's breath was still stirring the air, although he saw nothing out of the ordinary around him: same wilderness, same rocks, same sand. If someone had held a mirror in front of his face, Jacob would not have seen anything different there either, except for the circles of surprise in his eyes. "Surely the LORD is in this place," he said out loud, "—and I did not know it!" Shaken by what he had seen, he could not seem to stop talking. "How awesome is this place!" he went on. "This is none other than the house of God, and this is the gate of heaven."[1]

It was one of those dreams he could not have made up. It was one of those dreams that is so much more real than what ordinarily passes for real that trying to figure out "what really happened" involves a complete re-definition of terms. What is really real?

How do you know? Can you prove it? Even if Jacob could never find the exact place where the feet of that heavenly ladder came to earth—even if he could never find a single angel footprint in the sand—his life was changed for good. Having woken up to God, he would never be able to go to sleep again, at least not to the divine presence that had promised to be with him whether he could see it or not. What really happened? God knows. All Jacob knew was that he had to mark the spot.

Looking around for something that would do the trick, he spotted the obvious choice: his stone pillow, lying right where he had left it, although the sand around it was churned up from his unusual night's sleep. First he dug a sturdy footing for the stone. Then he stood it up, ladderlike, and set it into place. Then he poured oil on it and gave it a name: Bethel, House of God. Looking back at it as he walked away, he saw a stone finger rooted in the earth, pointing straight up through the sky.

Sitting in my salty, fragrant church back on the big island of Hawaii, I looked at the three stones pointing straight up through the sky and wondered how I had forgotten that the whole world is the House of God. Who had persuaded me that God preferred four walls and a roof to wide-open spaces? When had I made the subtle switch myself, becoming convinced that church bodies and buildings were the safest and most reliable places to encounter the living God?

I had loved plenty of churches in my life by then, beginning with a little white frame chapel in the Ohio countryside with apple trees in the churchyard. The pastor there was the first adult who looked me in the eyes and listened to what I said. He was the first to tuck God's pillow under my head. Later I loved a downtown Atlanta church where rows of Tiffany windows turned all the people inside faintly blue. With these people I learned how hard it was to do something as simple as loving our urban neighbors a fraction as much as we loved our true-blue selves. I loved the Washington National Cathedral, where presidents were laid to rest, pilgrims walked labyrinths, and rock doves occasionally roosted in the rafters. I loved tiny Grace-Calvary Episcopal Church in Clarkesville, Georgia, where for five and a half years I watched the wind bend the white pines from side to side through wavy clear glass windows while I celebrated communion with the faithful inside.

I encountered God in all of those places, which may explain why I began to spend more time in churches than I did in the wide, wide world. The physical boundaries of those houses were clear. The communities in them were identified. *Here is the church; here is the steeple; open the doors and see all the people.* I more or less knew what my job was inside those doors, and the rewards of doing it were clear. Engaging in ancient rituals with people as ordinary as I was, I watched their faces open to reveal night skies full of stars. Who would ever have imagined they carried so much around within them? Turning aside from everything else we could have been doing, we did things together in those sacred spaces that we did nowhere else in our lives: we named babies, we buried the dead, we sang psalms, we praised God for our lives. When we did, it was as if we were building a fire together, each of us adding something to the blaze so that the light and heat in our midst grew. Yet the light exceeded our fire, just as the warmth did. We did our parts, and then there was more. There was More.

Still, some of us were not satisfied with our weekly or biweekly encounters with God. We wanted more than set worship services or church work could offer us. We wanted more than planning scavenger hunts for the youth group, more than polishing silver

with the altar guild, more than serving on the outreach committee or rehearsing anthems with the choir. We wanted More. We
wanted a deeper sense of purpose. We wanted a stronger sense of
God's presence. We wanted more reliable ways both to seek and
to stay in that presence—not for an hour on Sunday morning or
Wednesday afternoon but for as much time as we could stand.

And yet the only way most of us knew to get that was to spend
more time in church. So we volunteered more, dreamed up more
programs, invited more people to more classes where we could read
more books. The minute we walked back out to our cars, many of
us could feel the same old gnawing inside. Once we left church, we
were not sure what to do anymore. We knew some things we could
do to feel close to God inside the church, but after we stepped into
the parking lot we lost that intimacy. The boundaries were not so
clear out there. Community was not so easy to find. Without Tiffany windows tinting them blue, people looked pretty much the
same. From the parking lot, they looked as ordinary as everything
else. The only More out there was more of the same.

That, at least, is how it looked to those of us who had forgotten
that the whole world is the House of God. Somewhere along the
line we bought—or were sold—the idea that God is chiefly interested in religion. We believed that God's home was the church,
that God's people knew who they were, and that the world was
a barren place full of lost souls in need of all the help they could
get. Plenty of us seized on those ideas because they offered us
meaning. Believing them gave us purpose and worth. They gave
us something noble to do in the midst of lives that might otherwise be invisible. Plus, there really are large swaths of the world
filled with people in deep need of saving.

The problem is, many of the people in need of saving are
in churches, and at least part of what they need saving from is

the idea that God sees the world the same way they do. What if the gravel of a parking lot looks as promising to God as the floorboards of a church? What if a lost soul strikes God as more reachable than a lifelong believer? What if God can drop a ladder absolutely anywhere, with no regard for the religious standards developed by those who have made it their business to know the way to God?

I could not possibly say.

Although I have spent a lot of my life in jobs that require me to speak for God, I am still reluctant to do it for all kinds of reasons. In the first place, I have discovered that people who want to speak to me about God generally have an agenda. However well-intentioned they may be, their speech tends to serve as a means to their own ends. They have a clear idea about how I should respond to what they are saying. They have a clear destination in mind for me, and nine times out of ten it is not some place I want to go.

In the second place, too much speech about God strikes me as disrespectful. In the Upanishads, God is described as "Thou Before Whom All Words Recoil." This sounds right to me. Anything I say about God will be inadequate. No matter how hard I try to say something true about God, the reality of God will eclipse my best words. The only reality I can describe with any accuracy is my own limited experience of what I think may be God: the More, the Really Real, the Luminous Web That Holds Everything in Place.

Even then, there is a good chance that my words will serve as an impediment for those who hear them. If "the Really Real" makes no sense to you, then you will have to find some way around that phrase before you can get on with your own description, which means that my speech about God has just done more to block your way than to open it. The only reason to accept such a risk is because most of us need to hear what other people say before we decide what to say about those same things ourselves. With a modicum of generosity, we can all pitch what we have on the fire and watch for the More to flame up. In the morning, when we wake up around a circle of glowing coals with warm stone pillows under our heads, there is always a chance that one of us will sit up and say, "Surely the LORD is present in this place, and I did not know it!"

When those words came out of Jacob's mouth, there was no temple in Jerusalem. Without one designated place to make their offerings, people were free to see the whole world as an altar. The divine could erupt anywhere, and when it did they marked the spot in any way they could, although there was no sense hanging around for long, since God stayed on the move. For years and years, the Divine Presence was content with a tent—a "tent of meeting," the Bible calls it—which was not where God lived full-time but where God camped out with people who were also on the move. God met them outside the tent, too, but the tent was the face-to-face place, the place where the presence of God was so intense that Moses was the only person who could stand it. When Moses came out of the tent of meeting, his face was so bright that he wore a veil over it in order not to scare the children.

The tent suited God just fine for hundreds of years. It suited God so well, in fact, that when King David proposed giving God a permanent address, God balked. "Are you the one to build me a house to live in?" God asked. "I have not lived in a house since the day I brought up the people of Israel from Egypt to this day, but I have been moving about in a tent and a tabernacle."[2] So David did not build God a temple. His son Solomon did, however, and from that day forth God's address was Mount Zion, Jerusalem.

Even today, two ruined temples later, people from around the world still go to Mount Zion to tuck their prayers into the foundation stones of God's old house.

As important as it is to mark the places where we meet God, I worry about what happens when we build a house for God. I am speaking no longer of the temple in Jerusalem but of the house of worship on the corner, where people of faith meet to say their prayers, because saying them together reminds them of who they are better than saying them alone. This is good, and all good things cast shadows. Do we build God a house so that we can choose when to go see God? Do we build God a house in lieu of having God stay at ours? Plus, what happens to the rest of the world when we build four walls—even four gorgeous walls—cap them with a steepled roof, and designate *that* the House of God? What happens to the riverbanks, the mountaintops, the deserts, and the trees? What happens to the people who never show up in our houses of God?

The people of God are not the only creatures capable of praising God, after all. There are also wolves and seals. There are also wild geese and humpback whales. According to the Bible, even trees can clap their hands. Francis of Assisi loved singing hymns with his brothers and sisters—who included not only Brother Bernard and Sister Clare, but also Brother Sun and Sister Moon. Francis could not have told you the difference between "the sacred" and "the secular" if you had twisted his arm behind his back. He read the world as reverently as he read the Bible. For him, a leper was as kissable as a bishop's ring, a single bird as much a messenger of God as a cloud full of angels. Francis had no discretion. He did not know where to draw the line between the church and the world. For this reason among others, Francis is remembered as a saint.

Of course, Francis also built a church. In a vision he had, as vivid as Jacob's vision of the divine ladder, God called upon Francis to re-build the church. Unsure what church God meant, Francis chose a ruined one near where he lived. He recruited all kinds of people to help him build it. Some of them just came to watch, and before they knew it were mixing cement. Others could not lift a single brick without help, but that worked out, since it led them to meet more people than they might have if they had been stronger. To most of them, building the church became more important than finishing it. Building it together gave people who were formerly invisible to each other meaning, purpose, and worth. When it was done at last, Francis's church did not stand as a shelter from the world; it stood as a reminder that the whole world was God's House.

I knew that when I was young, and then I forgot.

MY FIRST CHURCH was a field of broom grass behind my fam-ily's house in Kansas, where I spent days in self-forgetfulness. A small stream held swimmers, wigglers, skaters, and floaters, along with bumps of unseen things moving under the mud. When I blurred my eyes, the sun sparkling on the moving surface turned into a living quilt of light. Later, I found a magnolia tree in Georgia that offered high, medium, or low perches, depending on how far I could climb. My fear of falling made the ascent more vivid. When I had finally settled on a branch, my arms trembling from the haul, leaning back against the trunk felt as safe as lean-ing against my father. The huge white flowers leaked a scent much slighter than their size. When I bent to touch one, the cool, heavy petals fell to the ground like swooning birds.

Of course, I did other things as well. I went to school. I helped my mother with the dishes. I looked after my younger sisters.

I worked in the yard with my father. As I grew, I also smoked cigarettes with my friends, kissed boys in the backs of buses, and suffered the cruelties of the high school caste system. I became too tall too fast. My pale skin would not tan. I had no need of a brassiere until I was almost sixteen, by which time all the other girls seemed to have graduated from a course in voluptuousness that I did not have the resources to attend.

Fortunately, I had home remedies for the self-loathing that overtook me on a regular basis. After school I headed straight to the stables, where I kept a strawberry roan gelding named Frosty. He was always glad to see me. Although riding him was the point, I was just as happy to clean his stall. When I was through, he would stand very still as I lay my cheek against his, until the sweet hay smell of his breath revived me. In the evenings, I did my homework, wishing for more time with Melville's *Moby-Dick* and less with Euclid's geometry.

When I was sixteen, I joined a real church under my own steam. I was not then aware of the vast differences among churches. I thought God was God, and according to some of my friends I did not know the first thing about who He was or what He wanted from me. So I joined their church to find out, and quickly learned that my love of the world was misplaced. The church taught me that only God was worthy of my love, and that only the Bible could teach me about God. For the first time in my life, I was asked to choose between God and the world.

Like all who write what they remember, I am inventing the truth. But what I think I remember is that I learned in church to fear the world, or at least to suspect it. I learned that my body was of the world and that my bodily shame was appropriate. The kissing of boys should stop at once, my new teachers told me, as should all other flirtations with the temptations of the flesh. In the same way that the church was holier than the world, so was the spirit holier than the flesh. God so loved the world that He gave His only Son, but if the world had not been such a rotten place then that Son need not have died.

From many of those same churches I learned how important it was to love God and my neighbor as myself, to share what I had with those who had less, and to stand ready to lay down my life for my friends. I rose to those teachings like a seedling to the sun. They tapped my secret wish to become gallant. They gave me important things to do. If they also drove a wedge between me and the world I so loved, then I do not remember noticing that at the time. What I noticed was that I had found a church, a holy book, and a people of the book who promised me safety from worldly powers I did not even know were there. All I had to do was trust the God of the church more than I trusted the gods of the world, living the kind of in-but-not-of-the-world life that announced where my true allegiance lay.

From that rough start, I went on to learn that there are many different kinds of churches, many different ways to read the Bible, and many different ways that people of faith engage the world. Yet I never entirely escaped the subtle teaching that the world of the flesh is not to be trusted. As lovely, startling, or disturbing as that world may be, it is a world of appearances, not of truth—or so I was taught. Only the Bible contains the real truth, the truth that sets people free.

Fortunately, the Bible I set out to learn and love rewarded me with another way of approaching God, a way that trusts the union of spirit and flesh as much as it trusts the world to be a place of encounter with God. Like anyone else, I do some picking and choosing when I go to my holy book for proof that the world is holy too, but the evidence is there. People encounter God under shady oak trees, on riverbanks, at the tops of mountains, and in long stretches of barren wilderness. God shows up in whirlwinds, starry skies, burning bushes, and perfect strangers. When people want to know more about God, the son of God tells them to pay attention to the lilies of the field and the birds of the air, to women kneading bread and workers lining up for their pay.

Whoever wrote this stuff believed that people could learn as much about the ways of God from paying attention to the world as they could from paying attention to scripture. What is true is what happens, even if what happens is not always right. People can learn as much about the ways of God from business deals gone bad or sparrows falling to the ground as they can from reciting the books of the Bible in order. They can learn as much from a love affair or a wildflower as they can from knowing the Ten Commandments by heart.

This is wonderful news. I do not have to choose between the Sermon on the Mount and the magnolia trees. God can come to me by a still pool on the big island of Hawaii as well as at the altar of the Washington National Cathedral. The House of God stretches from one corner of the universe to the other. Sea monsters and ostriches live in it, along with people who pray in languages I do not speak, whose names I will never know.

I am not in charge of this House, and never will be. I have no say about who is in and who is out. I do not get to make the rules. Like Job, I was nowhere when God laid the foundations of the earth. I cannot bind the chains of the Pleiades or loose the cords of Orion. I do not even know when the mountain goats give birth, much less the ordinances of the heavens. I am a guest here, charged with serving other guests—even those who present themselves as my enemies. I am allowed to resist them, but as long as I trust in one God who made us all, I cannot act as if they are no kin to me. There is only one House. Human beings will either learn to live in it together or we will not survive to hear its sigh of relief when our numbered days are done.

In biblical terms, it is wisdom we need to live together in this world. Wisdom is not gained by *knowing* what is right. Wisdom is gained by *practicing* what is right, and noticing what happens when that practice succeeds and when it fails. Wise people do not have to be certain what they believe before they act. They are free to act, trusting that the practice itself will teach them what they need to know. If you are not sure what to think about washing feet, for instance, then the best way to find out is to practice washing a pair or two. If you are not sure what to believe about your neighbor's faith, then the best way to find out is to practice eating supper together. Reason can only work with the experience available to it. Wisdom atrophies if it is not walked on a regular basis.

Such wisdom is far more than information. To gain it, you need more than a brain. You need a body that gets hungry, feels pain, thrills to pleasure, craves rest. This is your physical pass into the accumulated insight of all who have preceded you on this earth. To gain wisdom, you need flesh and blood, because wisdom involves bodies—and not just human bodies, but bird bodies, tree bodies, water bodies, and celestial bodies. According to the Talmud, every blade of grass has its own angel bending over it, whispering, "Grow, grow."

How does one learn to see and hear such angels?

IF THERE IS A SWITCH to flip, I have never found it. As with Jacob, most of my visions of the divine have happened while I was busy doing something else. I did nothing to make them happen. They happened to me the same way a thunderstorm happens to me, or a bad cold, or the sudden awareness that I am desperately in love. I play no apparent part in their genesis. My only part is to decide how I will respond, since there is plenty I can do to make them go away, namely: 1) I can figure that I have had too much caffeine again; 2) I can remind myself that visions are not true in the same way that taxes and the evening news are true; or 3) I can return my attention to everything I need to get done today. These are only a few of the things I can do to talk myself out of living in the House of God.

Or I can set a little altar, in the world or in my heart. I can stop what I am doing long enough to see where I am, who I am there with, and how awesome the place is. I can flag one more gate to heaven—one more patch of ordinary earth with ladder marks on it—where the divine traffic is heavy when I notice it and even when I do not. I can see it for once, instead of walking right past it, maybe even setting a stone or saying a blessing before I move on to wherever I am due next.

Human beings may separate things into as many piles as we wish—separating spirit from flesh, sacred from secular, church from world. But we should not be surprised when God does not recognize the distinctions we make between the two. Earth is so thick with divine possibility that it is a wonder we can walk anywhere without cracking our shins on altars. Jacob's nowhere, about which he knew nothing, turned out to be the House of God. Even though his family had imploded, even though he had made his brother angry enough to kill him, even though he was a scoundrel from the word go—God decided to visit Jacob right where he was, though Jacob had not been right about anything so far and never would be. God gave Jacob vision, so Jacob could see the angels going up and down from earth to heaven, going about their business in the one and only world there is.

The vision showed Jacob something he did not know. He slept in the House of God. He woke at the gate of heaven. None of this was his doing. The only thing he did right was to see where he was and say so. Then he turned his pillow into an altar before he set off, praising the God who had come to him where he was.

2

The Practice of Paying Attention

REVERENCE

And in this he showed me something small, no bigger
than a hazelnut, lying in the palm of my hand, as it
seemed to me, and it was as round as a ball. I looked at
it with the eye of my understanding and thought: What
can this be? I was amazed that it could last, for I thought
that because of its littleness it would suddenly have fallen
into nothing. And I was answered in my understanding:
It lasts and always will, because God loves it; and thus
everything has being through the love of God.
                                        —*Julian of Norwich*

When I was seven, my family lived in Dublin, Ohio, for a
year. My father was a staff psychologist at the Veterans
Administration Hospital there. My mother was in charge of three
small children. I shared a bedroom with my sister Katy, while my

baby sister, Jennifer, slept in a crib in her own room. As hard as I have tried to remember the floor plan of that house, I cannot do it. All I can remember is the small wooden deck that opened off my parents' second-story bedroom, where I lay flat on my back the first time I saw a shower of falling stars.

I did not know then that they were called the Tears of Saint Lawrence, or that they returned every August. All I knew was that my father could be trusted when he told me there was something I needed to see. Some nights that meant looking through a large book of photographs from *Life* magazine that had arrived in that day's mail. Other nights it meant climbing in the car with him to go find the fire that was causing an orange glow in the sky. My father was such an accomplished chaser of fire engines that he could tell a brush fire from a house fire by the kind of smoke it sent up into the sky.

On the night I am remembering, he told me to pull the pale blue blanket off my bed and bring it to the deck. The air was sweet and cool. The sky bristled with stars. After my father had folded the blanket in half, he lay down on it with his hands folded behind his head. Katy and I lay down beside him, one under each elbow, where we could smell the Chapstick, tobacco, strong coffee smell of our father. If he explained what we were looking for, I do not remember that either. All I remember is lying there beside him looking into a sky I had never really looked into before, or at least never for so long.

When I breathed in, I seemed huge to myself. I felt as much a part of the sky as a feather on a bird's belly. When I breathed out, I became so small that I feared I might vanish. What was a seven-year-old girl, under that great weight of stars? When the first one fell, we all gasped and clutched at one another. *Did you see that? I did! Where did it go? To the far side of the moon.*

More and more stars fell as the night deepened. Some of them made clean arcs across the sky, while others disappeared before they had gone halfway. Watching them, I gained the understanding that the planet I was lying on looked like a star from somewhere else in the universe. It too might fall at any moment, taking me along with it. This understanding made my stomach flip even as it increased my investment in what was going on above my head. When my father woke me later, I could not believe I had fallen asleep. How do you fall asleep, with whole worlds plummeting before your eyes?

I learned reverence from my father. For him, it had nothing to do with religion and very little to do with God. I think it may have had something to do with his having been a soldier, since the exercise of reverence generally includes knowing your rank in the overall scheme of things. From him I learned by example that reverence was the proper attitude of a small and curious human being in a vast and fascinating world of experience. This world included people and places as well as things. Full appreciation of it required frequent adventures, grand projects, honed skills, and feats of daring. Above all, it required close attention to the way things worked, including one's own participation in their working or not working.

When I used one of my father's tools, he expected me to clean it with a wire brush and rub it down with a light coat of oil before putting it back where I had found it. My father's tools lasted forever. If I cut myself with one of them, he washed the wound with hydrogen peroxide and dabbed it with first-aid cream before covering it with a Band-Aid that was exactly the right size. My father's bandages were works of art.

In the days before guns carried the cultural weight they do now, he taught me how to clean a rifle properly. The gun was my own, a bolt-action Remington .22 with a wooden stock given to me by my Grandma Lucy, which I used to practice becoming the next Annie Oakley. All I ever shot were tin cans at the dump under close supervision, but in my father's house there was no using a gun without also knowing how to care for it.

The gun-cleaning ritual took place in his basement workshop, where there was room to line up everything we would need to do the job: a long metal rod one size smaller than the gun barrel, round patches of flannel, the can of solvent, a small brush that looked like a caterpillar, graphite, steel wool, fragrant oil, and several old cotton rags. These things were used in exactly this order.

First my father showed me how to check the shell chamber to make sure it was empty, how to set the safety, how to hold the gun so the muzzle always pointed away from us. Then, with the fingers of a surgeon, he attached one solvent-soaked patch to the end of the rod, sending it through the gun barrel with a sound that made my teeth hurt. He used the brush next, to loosen the gunk in the barrel. Then he let me run more cloth patches through until they came out clean. He used graphite last—to lubricate the barrel, he explained. Then he handed me the steel wool to scour the outside of the barrel. When I had finished, he ran an oil-soaked rag over the gun from breech to muzzle. Never touch any metal on the gun without cleaning your fingerprints off with a rag, my father said. Then he let me put the gleaming gun back in its case, ready for our next trip to the dump.

This ritual, among many others, introduced me to the practices that nourish reverence in a human life: paying attention, taking care, respecting things that can kill you, making the passage from fear to awe. Supreme Court justice Potter Stewart once said he could not define pornography, but he knew it when he saw it. Reverence is a little like that. It is difficult to define, but you know it when you feel it.

According to the classical philosopher Paul Woodruff, reverence is the virtue that keeps people from trying to act like gods. "To forget that you are only human," he says, "to think you can act like a god—this is the opposite of reverence."[1] While most of us live in a culture that reveres money, reveres power, reveres education and religion, Woodruff argues that true reverence cannot be for anything that human beings can make or manage by ourselves.

By definition, he says, reverence is the recognition of something greater than the self—something that is beyond human creation or control, that transcends full human understanding. God certainly meets those criteria, but so do birth, death, sex, nature, truth, justice, and wisdom. A Native American elder I know says that he begins teaching people reverence by steering them over to the nearest tree.

"Do you know that you didn't make this tree?" he asks them. If they say yes, then he knows that they are on their way.

Reverence stands in awe of something—something that dwarfs the self, that allows human beings to sense the full extent of our limits—so that we can begin to see one another more reverently as well. An irreverent soul who is unable to feel awe in the presence of things higher than the self is also unable to feel respect in the presence of things it sees as lower than the self, Woodruff says. This raises real questions about leaders, especially religious leaders, who cite reverence for what is good as their warrant for proclaiming whole populations of people evil.

Woodruff posts a number of cautions for those ready to draw a straight line between reverence and religion. While a church service may seem like the most natural place in the world to teach people how to be reverent, Woodruff says, a formal worship service can be a confusing place to look for reverence. "To begin with," he says, "worship is not always reverent; even the best forms of worship may be practiced without feeling (and therefore without reverence), and some forms of worship seem downright vicious."[2]

Some of the most reverent people I know decline to call themselves religious. For them, religion connotes belief. It means being able to say what you believe about God and why. It also means being able to hold your own in a debate with someone who believes otherwise. They, meanwhile, are not sure what they believe. They do not want to debate anyone. The longer they stand before the holy of holies, the less adequate their formulations of faith seem to them. Angels reach down and shut their mouths.

Reverence may take all kinds of forms, depending on what it is that awakens awe in you by reminding you of your true size. As I learned on that night of falling stars in Ohio, nature is a good place to start. Nature is full of things bigger and more powerful than human beings, including but not limited to night skies, oceans, thunderstorms, deserts, grizzly bears, earthquakes, and rain-swollen rivers. But size is not everything. Properly attended to, even a saltmarsh mosquito is capable of evoking reverence. See those white and black striped stockings on legs thinner than a needle? Where in those legs is there room for knees? And yet see how they bend, as the bug lowers herself to your flesh. Soon you and she will be blood kin. Your itch is the price of her life. Swat her if you must, but not without telling her she is beautiful first.

The easiest practice of reverence I know is simply to sit down somewhere outside, preferably near a body of water, and pay attention for at least twenty minutes. It is not necessary to take on the whole world at first. Just take the three square feet of earth on which you are sitting, paying close attention to everything that lives within that small estate. You might even decide not to kill anything for twenty minutes, including the saltmarsh mosquito that lands on your arm. Just blow her away and ask her please to go find someone else to eat.

With any luck, you will soon begin to see the souls in pebbles, ants, small mounds of moss, and the acorn on its way to becoming an oak tree. You may feel some tenderness for the struggling mayfly the ants are carrying away. If you can see the water, you may take time to wonder where it comes from and where it is going. You may even feel the beating of your own heart, that miracle of ingenuity that does its work with no thought or instruction from you. You did not make your heart, any more than you made a tree. You are a guest here. You have been given a free pass to this modest domain and everything in it.

If someone walks by or speaks to you, you may find that your power of attentiveness extends to this person as well. Even if you do not know him, you may be able to see his soul too, the one he thinks he has so carefully covered up. There is something he is working on in his life, the same way you are working on something. Can you see it in his face? You are related, even if you do not know each other's names.

If you cannot go outside, then find a pencil and a piece of paper and spend twenty minutes drawing your hand. Be sure you get the freckles right, the number of wrinkles around each knuckle. If you are old, marvel at what has happened to your skin. If you are young, find your lifeline. Pay attention to the scars, if you have them. On my left hand alone, I can see the gray shadow left by the pencil lead that broke off in my palm when I was nine. There is also a pale ellipse at the top of my index finger from a sewing accident in 1974. I was watching television at the time, when my program was interrupted for a special announcement from the White House. When Richard Nixon resigned, I was so stupefied that I cut off the end of my finger with my sewing scissors.

No one has time for this, of course. No one has time to lie on the deck watching stars, or to wonder how one's hand came to be, or to see the soul of a stranger walking by. Small wonder we are short on reverence. The artist Georgia O'Keeffe, who became famous for her sensuous paintings of flowers, explained her success by saying, "In a way, nobody sees a flower, really, it is so small, we haven't time—and to see takes time, like to have a friend takes time."[3]

The practice of paying attention really does take time. Most of us move so quickly that our surroundings become no more than the blurred scenery we fly past on our way to somewhere else. We pay attention to the speedometer, the wristwatch, the cell phone, the list of things to do, all of which feed our illusion that life is manageable. Meanwhile, none of them meets the first criterion for reverence, which is to remind us that we are not gods. If anything, these devices sustain the illusion that we might yet be gods—if only we could find some way to do more faster.

Reverence requires a certain pace. It requires a willingness to take detours, even side trips, which are not part of the original plan. Early in the Bible there is a story about Moses, who would turn out to be God's great partner in the liberation of the people Israel from bondage in Egypt. He was not that, yet. He was still a fugitive from justice, hiding out in the Arabian Desert to beat a murder rap back in Egypt.

Moses's life changed one day while he was tending his father-in-law's sheep. According to the storyteller, he had led the flock beyond the wilderness to Horeb, the mountain of God, when an angel of God appeared to him in a burning bush. The bush was not right in front of Moses, however. It must have been over to the side somewhere, because when Moses saw it, he said, "I must turn aside and look at this great sight, and see why the bush is not burned up."[4]

The bush required Moses to take a time-out, at least if he wanted to do more than glance at it. He could have done that. He could have seen the flash of red out of the corner of his eye, said, "Oh, how pretty," and kept right on driving the sheep. He did not know that it was an angel in the bush, after all. Only the storyteller knew that. Moses could have decided that he would come back tomorrow to see if the bush was still burning, when he had a little more time, only then he would not have been Moses. He would just have been a guy who got away with murder, without ever discovering what else his life might have been about.

What made him Moses was his willingness to turn aside. Wherever else he was supposed to be going and whatever else he was supposed to be doing, he decided it could wait a minute. He parked the sheep and left the narrow path in order to take a closer look at a marvelous sight. When he did, the storyteller says, God noticed. God dismissed the angel and took over the bush. "When the LORD saw that he had turned aside to see, God called to him out of the bush, 'Moses, Moses!'"

"Here I am," Moses said, and the rest is history. Before God asked Moses to do anything else, however, God asked Moses to take off his shoes. "Come no closer!" God warned him, not because the ground was hot but because it was holy. "Remove the sandals from your feet, for the place on which you are standing is holy ground."[5]

I have never been presented with a burning bush, but I did see a garden turn golden once. I must have been sixteen, earning summer spending money by keeping a neighbor's cats while she was away. The first time I let myself into the house, the fleas leapt on my legs like airborne piranha. Brushing them off as I opened cat food and cleaned litter pans, I finally fled through the back door with the bag of trash my employer had left for me to carry to the cans out back. I could hear the fleas inside flinging themselves against the plastic, so that it sounded as if a light rain were falling inside the bag.

I could not wait to be shed of it, which was why I was in a hurry. On my way to the cans, I passed a small garden area off to the left that was not visible from the house. Glancing at it, I got the whole dose of loveliness at once—the high arch of trees above, the mossy flagstones beneath, the cement birdbath, the cushiony bushes, the white wrought-iron chair—all lit by stacked planes of sunlight that turned the whole scene golden. It was like a door to another world. I had to go through it. I knew that if I did, then I would become golden too.

But first I had to ditch the bag. The fleas popped against the plastic as I hurried to the big aluminum garbage cans near the garage. Stuffing the bag into one of them, I turned back toward the garden, fervent to explore what I had only glimpsed in passing. When I got there, the light had changed. All that was left was a little overgrown sitting spot that no one had sat in for years. The smell of cat litter drifted from the direction of the garbage cans. The garden was no longer on fire.

"I think it pisses God off if you walk by the color purple in a field somewhere and don't notice it," says Shug Avery, one of the wise women in Alice Walker's book *The Color Purple*. I noticed the color gold, but I did not turn aside. I had a bag full of fleas to attend to. While I made that my first priority, the fire moved on in search of someone who would stop what she was doing, take off her shoes, and say, "Here am I."

Reverence for creation comes fairly easily for most people. Reverence for other people presents more of a challenge, especially if those people's lives happen to impinge upon your own. I live at the end of a dirt road in the country for a reason. I can see my nearest neighbor's house in the wintertime when all the trees are bare, but for the rest of the year we go about our business with no visual confirmation of each other's presence. We like each other very much. We also like our distance from each other. I cannot speak for him, but I know that I have an easier time loving humankind than I do loving particular human beings.

Particular human beings hug my bumper in rush-hour traffic and shoot birds at me when I tap my brakes. Particular human beings drop my carefully selected portabella mushrooms into the bottom of my grocery bag and toss cans of beans on top of them. They talk on their cell phones while I am having a nice quiet lunch at Blimpie's; they talk on their cell phones while I am waiting to pay them for my gas; they talk on their cell phones while I am trying to step past them on the sidewalk. Particular human beings rarely do things the way I think they should do them, and when they prevent me from doing what I think I should be doing, then I can run short on reverence for them.

One remedy for my condition is to pay attention to them when I can, even when they are in my way. Just for a moment, I look for the human being instead of the obstacle. That boy who is crushing my portabellas does not know the first thing about mushrooms. He is, what, sixteen years old? With such a bad case of acne that it has to hurt when he lays his face on his pillow at night. His fingernails are bitten to the quick. He is working so hard to impress the pretty young cashier that it is no wonder he does not see me. But I see him, and for just a moment he is more than the bag boy. He is a kid with his own demons, his own bad skin and budding lusts. I do not want too much information about any of this, but I can at least let him be more than a bit player in my drama. I pay attention to him, and the fist in my chest lets go.

"Heavy stuff on the bottom," I say, so that the kid looks at me. "Take it easy on my mushrooms, okay?" He cocks his head, grins.

"These things are *mushrooms*?" he says, hauling them out of the bottom of the bag. "I wouldn't eat one of those on a bet."

I have a variation of this practice that I do on the subway, at least if I have a pair of sunglasses with me. From behind the veils of my dark lenses, I study the particular human beings sitting around me: the girl with the fussy baby, the guy with the house paint all over his jeans, the couple holding hands, the teenager keeping time with both knees while he listens to music so loud it leaks from his headphones. Every one of these people has come from somewhere and is going somewhere, the same way I am. While I am sitting here thinking I am at the center of this subway scene and they are on the edges, they are sitting there at the center of their own scenes with me on their edges. Every one of them is dealing with something, the same way I am. We are breathing the same air, for this little time at least. Sometimes I say the Lord's Prayer under my breath while I look from one of them to the next, but this is optional. Paying attention to them has already shifted my equilibrium. For all I know, one of them is practicing reverence on me.

It is not necessary to invent new practices, of course. Praying for thine enemies is as old as the Sermon on the Mount. So is the laying on of hands, the anointing of the sick, and the bathing of the dead. If you have ever done any of these things, then you know that it is just about impossible to do them without suffering a sudden onset of reverence. They accomplish this, I think, by giving you something so important to do that you are entirely captured by the present moment for once. For once, you are not looking through things, or around them, toward the next thing, which will become see-through in its turn. For once, you are giving yourself entirely to what is right in front of you, and what is right in front of you is returning the favor so that reverence is all but unavoidable.

Simone Weil was a French Jew who died of hunger during World War II. She did not have to die of hunger. Her family was wealthy, she was extremely well educated, and she never fell into the clutches of the Nazis. She remained so affected by what was happening to other, less-protected, people under the Third Reich that she decided to live as they lived. She worked in factories when she could have been teaching in schools. She lived on tinned rations when she could have been eating fresh eggs cooked in butter.

"The great trouble in human life is that looking and eating are two different operations," she writes in *Waiting for God*. Human beings have a hard time regarding anything beautiful without wanting to devour it. A child may love looking at a shiny red apple so much that she hates the idea of biting into it, but her appetite will win out. What good is looking at a lovely thing when you can take it inside of you? The same instinct drives compulsive shoppers, promiscuous lovers, and petty thieves. "It may be that vice, depravity, and crime are nearly always, or even perhaps always, in their essence, attempts to eat beauty, to eat what we should only look at," Weil guesses, before quoting one of her favorite passages from the Upanishads. Two winged companions, two birds, are on the branch of a tree. One eats the fruit; the other looks at it. "These two birds," Weil says, "are the two parts of our soul."[6]

Weil's second bird guided her relationship with the church. Although she grew up a secular Jew, she was drawn so strongly to the sacramental life of the church that her desire for baptism became almost overwhelming to her. Yet she declined to be baptized, saying that she could not seek her own soul's safety in any church that denied salvation to those who did not belong to it. This meant that she spent the rest of her short life regarding the bread and wine of Holy Communion without ever eating them. Regarding them was enough for her, even as they strengthened her resolve to stay hungry with those who were hungry, to remain outside the safety of the church with those who were outside. Weil died in an English sanatorium on August 29, 1943, at the age of thirty-four.

Regarded properly, anything can become a sacrament, by which I mean an outward and visible sign of an inward and spiritual connection. Take food, for example. Before I moved to the country, I bought my chicken, eggs, and potatoes at the grocery store, along with my bread, celery, and milk. I like white meat, so boneless breasts frequently showed up in my shopping basket, along with the occasional rotisserie chicken. When I moved to rural north Georgia, I inadvertently moved to one of the largest chicken-producing areas in the country. At night, I drove by huge chicken barns lit up inside so that I could see the hundreds of white chickens crowded inside. By day, I ended up behind loud trucks stacked with wire cages full of those same chickens on their way to be slaughtered.

I think the idea is to put them in a state of shock so that they do not struggle so much when they arrive at the abattoir. The chickens are unprotected on the trucks. In bitter cold, they huddle inside the cages while the wind whips their white feathers into a cloud behind the truck. The first time I drove five miles with those feathers glancing off my windshield, the feathers became sacraments for me. I got the connection between them and boneless chicken breasts in a way I had never gotten it before. I saw what dies so that I may live, and while I did not stop eating chicken meat, I began cooking it and eating it with unprecedented reverence.

Other sacraments take more work. But if you are paying attention, even a mail-order catalog can become a sacrament. First, there are the people who produced the catalog—the designers, the photographers, the models, and the copyeditors—along with the people who produced the goods inside. Some of those people live in Mexico and others in the Philippines. In China, where cashmere goats are bred to produce sweaters for American consumers, traditional grasslands are so overgrazed that thousands of square miles turn to desert each year. If you could lay a laminated map of the world on the floor and put a pin in every place where something in that mail-order catalog came from, you might be amazed at how prickly the map became.

Then there is the paper and the ink. I do not know where the ink in all my catalogs came from, but I know something about the paper. Four miles from my house, there was once a sizable forest of pines. White-tailed deer lived there, along with skunks, raccoons, and a flock of wild turkeys. Then one day the loggers came. It took them a couple of weeks to reduce the forest to stumps, but they did it. When I drove by, I could smell the sap as strongly as if it had leaked on my hands.

Pine is the cheapest, most renewable source of pulpwood for paper. I use paper, and I know it has to come from somewhere. I just hate thinking that a whole forest came down for one run of a mail-order catalog, especially since I saw so many copies of that catalog in the trash at the post office. From there, they will go to the landfill, where wastepaper is the number one problem. The sacrament of the catalog creates more than reverence in me; it creates painful awareness of my part in the felling of the forest. It weaves me into the web of cause and effect, reminding me of my place in the overall scheme of things.

I understand why people snort at thoughts like these. I have laughed the same kind of laugh when people start talking earnestly about things I would rather not talk about. Reverence can be a pain. It is a lot easier to make chicken salad if you have never been stuck behind a chicken truck. It is easier to order a cashmere sweater if you do not know about the Chinese goats. And yet, these doors open onto the divine as surely as showers of falling stars do. To open only the doors with stars on them while leaving shut the doors covered with chicken feathers is to live half a life, with half a heart.

As painful as reverence can sometimes be, it can also heal. I know for a fact that it is possible to survive great grief by hauling a mattress outside on a clear night and lying flat on your back under the belly of the sky. Holding a baby also works, or a stunned hummingbird if you are lucky enough to find one. I knew a woman once who was not sure she wanted to go on living. She was old. She lived alone. She was afraid to go to sleep at night for fear that she would not wake up in the morning, so she lay in her bed waiting for the sun to come up before she dared to shut her eyes.

Then someone who loved her suggested that as long as she was awake, she might as well start listening for the first bird that sang each morning. Before long, the sound of that bird became the bell that woke her heart to life again. She named the bird. She discovered what such birds like to eat and put feeders full of seed in her yard. Other birds came, and she learned their names as well. She began to collect birdhouses, which she hung from the rafters of her porch until she became the mayor of an entire bird village. She still does not sleep well, but she is no longer afraid of her life.

The practice of paying attention is as simple as looking twice at people and things you might just as easily ignore. To see takes time, like having a friend takes time. It is as simple as turning off the television to learn the song of a single bird. Why should anyone do such things? I cannot imagine—unless one is weary of crossing days off the calendar with no sense of what makes the last day different from the next. Unless one is weary of acting in what feels more like a television commercial than a life. The practice of paying attention offers no quick fix for such weariness, with guaranteed results printed on the side. Instead, it is one way into a different way of life, full of treasure for those who are willing to pay attention to exactly where they are.

This chapter began with a passage from Dame Julian of Norwich, a fourteenth-century English visionary who was thirty years old when she received the first of several revelations of divine love. She thought she was dying. For three days she had been mortally ill. On the fourth night a priest came to give her last rites. As she was looking at the cross he held in front of her face to comfort her as she died, all of her pain suddenly vanished and she felt as well as she had ever been. In short order, she saw two things: the face of Jesus, with blood flowing down his face from his crown of thorns, and something small, no bigger than a hazelnut, lying in her hand.

"What can this be?" she wondered to herself.

"It is everything which is made," was the answer she received. She held all creation in her hand, as round as a nut. Looking at it, she understood three things: that God made it, that God loves it, and that God preserves it. Fifteen years and fifteen visions later, she was still asking God what it all meant when the answer came to her: "What, do you wish to know your Lord's meaning in this thing? Know it well, love was his meaning. Who reveals it to you?

Love. What did he reveal to you? Love. Why does he reveal it to you? For love. Remain in this, and you will know more of the same. But you will never know different, without end."[7]

Julian never said so, but I doubt she ever looked at as much as a peppercorn the same way again. How could she, once God had shown her the whole world in the palm of her hand? Paying attention to it, she learned how God paid attention to her. Holding it, she learned how God held her.

Like all the other practices in this book, paying attention requires no equipment, no special clothes, no greens fees or personal trainers. You do not even have to be in particularly good shape. All you need is a body on this earth, willing to notice where it is, trusting that even something as small as a hazelnut can become an altar in this world.

3

The Practice of Wearing Skin

INCARNATION

> People ask me: why do you write about food, and eating
> and drinking? Why don't you write about the struggle for
> power and security, and about love, the way the others
> do? The easiest answer is to say that, like most other
> humans, I am hungry.
>
> —*M. F. K. Fisher*

O nce, when I was a guest speaker at a church in Alabama, I
decided to take a look around the sanctuary before the service began. It was a grand old Episcopal church, circa 1920, with
Tiffany-style stained-glass windows and a striking mural of Jesus
emerging from his tomb over the altar. Since I was a good forty-
five minutes early I had the place to myself, except for a member
of the altar guild who was polishing silver in the sacristy. She
was the kind of woman who helped me feel inadequate simply by

being so pulled together. Her clothes were expensive. Every hair on her pretty head was in place. I could see her manicured fingernails flying as she polished a silver chalice with a soft gray rag.

"Hey," I said.

"Hey," she said. This is how we greet one another in the South. "Hey there" is a common variation, which Northerners sometimes misunderstand as an accusation of some sort, as in "Hey you! What do you think you are doing?" The inflection is key. Like Mandarin or Gaelic, Southern dialect requires a good ear. "Hey" means "Hello, I see you standing there." Unless the person addressing you says "Hey, how are you?" she does not want to hear how you are doing. She just wants to meet the minimum standard for being thought a polite person.

"Hey," the perfect, polite woman said. Then she went back to polishing silver and I went back to checking out the church.

Once I had adjusted the height of the podium and the angle of the microphone, I walked up behind the altar so I could see the mural up close. It was a real masterpiece. Did John Singer Sargent do altarpieces? Above my head, Jesus was stepping out of his tomb looking as limber as a ballet dancer with his arms raised in blessing. Roman soldiers slumped in sleep on either side of the tomb with Easter lilies blooming under their noses. Except for a white cloth swaddling his waist, Jesus was naked. His skin was the color of a pink rose. His limbs were flooded with light.

The painting was so realistic that I leaned in for a closer look. I could not remember ever having seen so much of Jesus's skin before, especially in church. I felt protective of him, all exposed like that in such a public place. But I could see the artist's point. Even in Jesus's most transcendent moment, the moment that set him apart from the rest of humankind, he remained recognizably one of us. He came back wearing skin. He did not leave his body behind.

In his presence, I felt overdressed, overdefended. What was I hiding? What did he have that I was missing? Something was missing in the painting as well, but I could not think what it was. The wounds in his feet, his hands, and his side were clear but not gory. His upraised arms looked thin but strong. Staring at his underarms, I realized with a start why he looked so ethereal. Jesus had no body hair.

"It's beautiful, isn't it?" The pulled-together woman in the sacristy was watching me through the open door.

"It surely is that," I said, "but did you ever notice that he has no body hair? He has the underarms of a six-year-old. His chest is as smooth as a peach." Her manicured fingernails stopped moving as the smile froze on her face.

"I can't believe you're saying this to me," she said without moving her red lips. "I just can't believe you're saying this to me."

This happens to me a lot. Since at least one of the reasons I remain Christian is because of the seriousness with which Christian tradition honors flesh and blood, I am always surprised at how easy it is for me to become an oaf—usually by saying something obvious about the human body in the presence of those devoted to the soul. In the case at hand, it was saying something about Jesus's body that got me in trouble, but I can just as easily descend into oafdom by saying something about my own body or the bodies of other people when we are supposed to be speaking of spiritual things.

For instance, I can say that I think it is important to pray naked in front of a full-length mirror sometimes, especially when you are full of loathing for your body. Maybe you think you are too heavy. Maybe you have never liked the way your hipbones stick out. Do your breasts sag? Are you too hairy? It is always something. Then again, maybe you have been sick, or come through some surgery that has changed the way you look. You have gotten glimpses of your body as you have bathed or changed clothes, but so far maintaining your equilibrium has depended upon staying covered up as much as you can. You have even discovered how to shower in the dark, so that you may have to feel what you presently loathe about yourself but you do not have to look at it.

This can only go on so long, especially for someone who officially believes that God loves flesh and blood, no matter what kind of shape it is in. Whether you are sick or well, lovely or irregular, there comes a time when it is vitally important for your spiritual health to drop your clothes, look in the mirror, and say, "Here I am. This is the body-like-no-other that my life has shaped. I live here. This is my soul's address." After you have taken a good look around, you may decide that there is a lot to be thankful for, all things considered. Bodies take real beatings. That they heal from most things is an underrated miracle. That they give birth is beyond reckoning.

When I do this, I generally decide that it is time to do a better job of wearing my skin with gratitude instead of loathing. No matter what I think of my body, I can still offer it to God to go on being useful to the world in ways both sublime and ridiculous. At the very least, I can practice a little reverence right there in front of the mirror, taking some small credit for standing there unguarded for once. This is no small thing, in a culture so confused about the body that most Americans cannot separate the physical from the sexual. Comment on the beauty of a child's body and you risk being viewed as a potential predator. Make an observation about your own and you risk being called seductive.

One of the most remarkable conversations I have ever had about the physics of divine love took place in a far country, where a male colleague and I were involved in a monthlong service project. We were done with our work for the day. We were enjoying a good dinner over a bottle of equally good wine. After two glasses of it, the conversation turned to our physical attraction—not for each other, but for God. Sometimes, he said, when he was preaching a sermon he really cared about, he grew so aware of God's presence that he became physically aroused. He rose to God's presence as to the presence of the Beloved. His sense of spiritual intimacy flowed straight into his sense of physical intimacy. They were not two but one. He was not two but one. He and God were not two but one.

Inspired by his divine audacity, I allowed as how I had experienced the same thing myself, although with different physical equipment. Sometimes when I was praying, my body could not tell the difference between that and making love. Every cell in my body rose to the occasion, so that I felt the prayer prick my breasts and warm my belly, lifting every hair on my body in full alert. Body and soul were not two but one. I was not two but one. God and I were not two but one.

I understand why conversations like these are rare. I just hope they do not become extinct. "There is only one love," wrote Teresa of Avila, the sixteenth-century nun whose rapturous encounters with God sometimes left her unconscious with bliss. As she and her fellow religious have testified throughout the ages, God does not often enter the library of the soul with a ghost key and start reading psalms. God is much more likely to head straight to the bedroom.

"O stormy, violent, burning, surging love who do not permit that one should think something other than you," Bernard of Clairvaux once wrote of this amorous God, ". . . you tear down orders, pay no heed to ancestry, know no measure. Propriety, reason, modesty, counsel, judgment—all these you make your prisoners."[1]

I am not sure when Christian tradition lost confidence in the body, but I have some guesses. Although Jesus was a Jew, many of his earliest interpreters were Greeks, who divided body and soul in ways that he did not. Descartes did not help matters by opposing nature and reason in his philosophy. Then along came the Protestant Reformation, with its deep suspicion of physical pleasure, followed by Freud's dark insights into human sexuality. Add to that the modern scientific reduction of the body to biological matter, overlaid by Victoria's Secret ads, and it is small wonder that so many of us are uncomfortable in our flesh.

Yet here we sit, with our souls tucked away in this marvelous luggage, mostly insensible to the ways in which every spiritual practice begins with the body. Our bodies have shaped our views of the world, just as the world has shaped our views of our bodies. Each of us has a unique body "signature," which consists not only of our distinctive physical characteristics but also of our posture, our gait, our way of using our hands. The moment I come into a room, you can tell that I was 5'10" in the eighth grade. All these years later, it is still difficult for me to stand up straight. To square my shoulders requires an act of conscious will, since that only makes me taller.

Shake my hand and you can tell even more about me. I shake like a man, as best I can. When someone grasps the middle three fingers of my hand and gives me a lady shake, I feel dismissed. I know my hands are cold in the winter, which is why I rub my right one on my pants leg several times before I greet someone in December. Each of us has not only a set temperature but also a kinetic energy about us, a distinctive way of being physical that tells others more about us than anything we say.

"It is easier to lie with the lips than with the body," goes an old proverb, which also goes a long way toward explaining why many of us are so reticent about our flesh. It is not easy being so *revealed* to every passerby, who can often read us better than we can read ourselves simply by watching the way we walk, sit, or eat. Our bodies are prophets. They know when things are out of whack and they say so, although most of us welcome their news about as warmly as the people of Jerusalem welcomed Jeremiah's. We would rather lock up our bodies than listen to what they have to say. Where Christians are concerned, this leaves us in the peculiar position of being followers of the Word Made Flesh who neglect our own flesh or—worse—who treat our bodies with shame and scorn.

I came late to the understanding that God loved all of me—not just my spirit but also my flesh. Like many young people raised in the fifties, I grew up with a lot of questions and unearned shame about my ripening body, which was not ripening in a way that matched any of the movie posters or *Playboy* magazines by which female beauty was measured in those days. Barbie dolls did not help. When the movie *Barbarella* came out, starring Jane Fonda in a black vinyl bodysuit, I gained a new nickname meant to mortify me, which it did.

When understanding finally came—not by reason but by faith—the first thing I understood was that it was not possible to trust that God loved all of me, including my body, without also trusting that God loved all bodies everywhere. God loved the bodies of hungry children and indentured women along with the bodies of sleek athletes and cigar-smoking tycoons. While we might not have one other thing in common, we all wore skin. We all had breath and beating hearts. Most of us had wept, although not for the same reasons. Few of our bodies worked the way we wanted them to. The vast majority of us were afraid of dying.

One of the truer things about bodies is that it is just about impossible to increase the reverence I show mine without also increasing the reverence I show yours. However differently you and I may conceive the world, God, or one another, physical reality is something we can usually agree on. When the temperature drops below 32 degrees, I am as cold as whoever happens to be standing next to me. When I see someone run into a piece of furniture, catching the corner of a table right in the thigh, my own thigh hurts in that exact same place. When I am sitting next to someone in a meeting and our stomachs growl at the same time, we both shift in our seats, unable to ignore a connection more fundamental than knowing each other's names. When I watch a perfect stranger open her mouth for a bite of Key lime pie at my favorite Mexican restaurant, my mouth starts watering without my permission.

My body is what connects me to all of these other people. Wearing my skin is not a solitary practice but one that brings me into communion with all these other embodied souls. It is what we have most in common with one another. In Christian teaching, followers of Jesus are called to honor the bodies of our neighbors as we honor our own. In his expanded teaching by example, this includes leper bodies, possessed bodies, widow and orphan bodies, as well as foreign bodies and hostile bodies—none of which he shied away from. Read from the perspective of the body, his ministry was about encountering those whose flesh was discounted by the world in which they lived.

What many of us miss, in our physical dis-ease, is that our bodies remain God's best way of getting to us.

DEEP SUFFERING makes theologians of us all. The questions people ask about God in Sunday school rarely compare with the questions we ask while we are in the hospital. This goes for those stuck in the waiting room as well as those in actual beds. To love someone who is suffering is to learn the visceral definition of *pathetic*: 1) affecting or exciting emotion, especially the tender emotions, as pity or sorrow; 2) so inadequate as to be laughable or contemptible. To spend one night in real pain is to discover depths of reality that are roped off while everything is going fine. *Why me? Why now? Why this?*

These are natural questions to ask when you are in pain, but they are just as relevant when you are in pleasure. Who deserves the way a warm bath feels on a cold night after a hard day's work? Who has earned the smell of a loved one, embracing you on your first night back home? To hold a sleeping child in your arms can teach you more about the meaning of life than any ten books on the subject. To lie in the yard at night looking up at the stars can grant you entrance into divine mysteries that elude you inside the house.

The daily practice of incarnation—of being in the body with full confidence that God speaks the language of flesh—is to discover a pedagogy that is as old as the gospels. Why else did Jesus spend his last night on earth teaching his disciples to wash feet and share supper? With all the conceptual truths in the universe at his disposal, he did not give them something to think about together when he was gone. Instead, he gave them concrete things to do—specific ways of being together in their bodies—that would go on teaching them what they needed to know when he was no longer around to teach them himself.

After he was gone, they would still have God's Word, but that Word was going to need some new flesh. The disciples were going to need something warm and near that they could bump into on a regular basis, something so real that they would not be able to intellectualize it and so essentially untidy that there was no way they could ever gain control over it. So Jesus gave them things they could get their hands on, things that would require them to get close enough to touch one another. In the case of the meal, he gave them things they could smell and taste and swallow. In the case of the feet, he gave them things to wash that were attached to real human beings, so that they could not bend over them without being drawn into one another's lives.

Wow. How did you get that scar? Does it hurt when I touch it? No, really, they're not ugly. You should see mine. Yours just have a few more miles on them. Do you ever feel like you can't go any further? Like you just want to stop right here and let this be it? I know, I can't stop either. It's weird, isn't it? You follow him and you follow him, thinking that any minute now the sky is going to crack open, and you're going to see the face of God. Then he hands you his basin and his towel, and it turns out that it's all about feet, you know? Yours, mine, his. Feet, for God's sake.

I am making this up, of course. Read the Bible commentaries and they will tell you that the foot washing in John's gospel is an eschatological sign of Jesus's descent into flesh before his exaltation to God's right hand, or a symbolic representation of first-century baptismal theology. But I will tell you this. After years of watching bodies being dug out of craters in Manhattan and caves in Afghanistan, after the body counts coming from southeast Asia, Gaza, and Iraq, most of us could use a reminder that God does not come to us beyond the flesh but in the flesh, at the hands of a teacher who will not be spiritualized but who goes on trusting the embodied sacraments of bread, wine, water, and feet.

"Do this," he said—not *believe* this but *do* this—"in remembrance of me."

Duke ethicist Stanley Hauerwas finds most Christians far too spiritual in the practice of their faith. Christianity "is not a set of beliefs or doctrines one believes in order to be a Christian," he says, "but rather Christianity is to have one's body shaped, one's habits determined, in such a way that the worship of God is unavoidable."[2] In our embodied life together, the words of our doctrines take on flesh. If one of our orthodox beliefs has no corporeal value, if we cannot come up with a single consequence it has for our embodied life together, then there is good reason to ask why we should bother with it at all. The issue Hauerwas raises is not whether there is any such thing as purely spiritual holiness, but "whether there is anything beside the body that can be sanctified."[3]

In far more pungent language, Daniel Berrigan once said, "It all comes down to this: Whose flesh are you touching and why? Whose flesh are you recoiling from and why? Whose flesh are you burning and why?"[4]

Such questions strike below the radar screen of the intellect, where far too many questions of faith are both argued and answered. When I hear people talk about what is wrong with organized religion, or why their mainline churches are failing, I hear about bad music, inept clergy, mean congregations, and preoccupation with institutional maintenance. I almost never hear about the intellectualization of faith, which strikes me as a far greater danger than anything else on the list. In an age of information overload, when a vast variety of media delivers news faster than most of us can digest—when many of us have at least two e-mail addresses, two telephone numbers, and one fax number—the last thing any of us needs is more information about God. We need the practice of incarnation, by which God saves the lives of those whose intellectual assent has turned as dry as dust, who have run frighteningly low on the bread of life, who are dying to know more God in their bodies. Not more *about* God. *More God.*

Sometimes, when people ask me about my prayer life, I describe hanging laundry on the line. After a day of too much information about almost everything, there is such blessed relief in the weight of wet clothes, causing the wicker basket to creak as I carry it out to the clothesline. Every time I bend down to shake loose a piece of laundry, I smell the grass. I smell the sun. Above all, I smell clean laundry. This is something concrete that I have accomplished, a rarity in my brainy life of largely abstract accomplishments.

Most of the laundry belongs to my husband, Ed, who can go through more clothes in a week than most toddlers. Hanging his laundry on the line becomes a labor of love. I hang each T-shirt like a prayer flag, shaking it first to get the wrinkles out and then pinning it to the line with two wooden clothespins. Even the clothespins give me pleasure. I add a prayer for the trees from which these clothespins came, along with the Penley Corporation of West Paris, Maine, which is still willing to make them from wood instead of colored plastic.

Since I am a compulsive person, I go to some trouble to impose order on the lines of laundry: handkerchiefs first, then jockey shorts, then T-shirts, then jeans. If I sang these clothes, the musical notes they made would lead me in a staccato, downward scale. The socks go all in a row at the end like exclamation points. All day long, as I watch the breeze toss these clothes in the wind, I imagine my prayers spinning away over the tops of the trees. This is good work, this prayer. This is good prayer, this work.

So is digging in the garden, cleaning the chicken pens, washing the potatoes, doing the dishes. I know there are people who would give anything to do these things, people whose bodies have become too numb, too busy, too old or painful to do them. These are the practices that sustain life—not only my life and the lives entwined with mine, but the lives of all living beings. When I haul water, I am in instant communion with all other haulers of water around the world. We may have little else in common, but we all know the deep pleasure of being water-bearers. To deliver water for drinking, for cooking, for washing, for bathing: this is what muscles are for. To watch a thirsty creature dip its head to the bucket and drink: I am happy to sweat for this.

Above all, I am happy for practices that bring me back to my body, where the operative categories are not "bad" and "good" but "dead" and "alive." As hard as I have tried to be good all my life—as hard as I try to be good even now—my heart leans more and more toward that which gives life, whether it is conventionally good or not. There are times when dancing on tables grants more life than kneeling in prayer. More to the point, there are times when dancing on tables is the most authentic prayer in reach, even if it pocks the table and clears the room.

Maybe I have watched *Zorba the Greek* too many times, but I find myself rebelling against any religious definition of goodness that leaves the body behind. When I came upon the words of the following hymn in a seminary chapel two summers ago, I could not believe my eyes.

Good is the flesh that the Word has become,
    good is the birthing, the milk in the breast,
    good is the feeding, caressing and rest,
    good is the body for knowing the world,
Good is the flesh that the Word has become.

Good is the body for knowing the world,
    sensing the sunlight, the tug of the ground,
    feeling, perceiving, within and around,

good is the body, from cradle to grave,
Good is the flesh that the Word has become.

Good is the body from cradle to grave,
    growing and ageing, arousing, impaired,
    happy in clothing or lovingly bared,
    good is the pleasure of God in our flesh.
Good is the flesh that the Word has become.

Good is the pleasure of God in our flesh,
    longing in all, as in Jesus, to dwell,
    glad of embracing, and tasting, and smell,
    good is the body, for good and for God,
Good is the flesh that the Word has become.

The hymn writer is Brian Wren, one of the church's most gifted musicians. In the case of this hymn, he is also one of the bravest. I never thought I would be able to sing "milk in the breast" in church, much less "good is the feeding, caressing and rest." I do not recall ever being told that my flesh is good in church, or that God takes pleasure in it. Yet this is the central claim of the incarnation—that God trusted flesh and blood to bring divine love to earth.

In the same chapel where I found this hymn, I led a workshop called "Embodied Holiness," which drew a full house of thirty-four women and six men, both clergy and lay. Like me, they were interested in exploring *how* they knew what they knew about God, and also like me, they confessed a cognitive bias, at least in polite company. Most of us knew what we knew about God from the historical creeds of the church, from studying the Oxford Annotated Bible with other people, from reading books by favorite authors, and from listening to certain people speak. At least that was how we *thought* we knew what we knew about God.

Then one morning we explored the Beatitudes, only instead of talking about them we decided to embody them. In groups of five or six, people went off to different corners of the large room with one verse that they were charged with bringing to life. The assignment was to arrange the members of the group into a tableau that embodied the Beatitude without using any words, and then to show that Beatitude to the rest of us.

As you can imagine, the resistance to doing this was enormous, verging on panic in a couple of cases. We were adults, after all. Kids *act* things out. Adults *discuss* them. Plus, most of us had memorized the Beatitudes. We could say them in our sleep, and we had all heard more sermons on them than any of us wanted to count. I watched a couple of seasoned pastors eye the door to see if they could get out before anyone stopped them. One priest volunteered to be the corpse in her Beatitude so that she would not have to do anything but lie there. ("Blessed are those who mourn, for they shall be comforted.") In the end everyone stayed put, thanks largely to a number of emerging group leaders who I am pretty sure were all eldest children.

After about fifteen minutes, the groups began to perform. We did not go in order, so the first Beatitude was about those who hunger and thirst for righteousness. Five women came out, arranged themselves in a circle facing out and turned into a bunch of baby birds all squalling for food. They used their hands to make big beaks, so that they were mostly mouths. One looked like she was going to die if she did not get something to eat real soon. She was barely peeping. Then the momma bird showed up and flew around the circle with food in her own beak, filling each of her babies in turn. They rose and flapped as she approached. They grew right before our eyes. Then one by one the beaks turned to wings and the babies *flew*.

It was so strong that no one spoke. The five women moved out of the center of the room as another group took their place. We watched another stunning Beatitude, and then another. Finally the "Blessed Are Those Who Mourn" group came out—all women again—and arranged themselves around the woman who had volunteered to lie dead on the ground. A second woman sat down and cradled the first woman's head in her lap. Two others knelt beside her and two others stood over them until they made a sort of cathedral over the dead woman's body. Everyone was touching someone so that they were all linked together, but unlike the first group no one moved. The women just held that pose, so full of love and grief, until a sob rose right out of the midst of them.

Those of us watching did not know what to do. Was that the end? That sad, sad sound could have been planned, but it did not sound planned. What was going on? Was this still pretend or was this real? Those of us watching the tableau froze just like those who were in it. Then, when the whole room was as still as a grave, the body of the woman on the floor began to heave. As her soft sobbing grew louder, the other women bent over it. Then one of them began to weep, and another gave a small, strangled yelp until the whole tableau was heaving ever so gently over the body of the dead woman who had come back to life.

I cannot tell you how long it lasted—a minute, an hour—but at some point the women straightened up and wiped their eyes while the rest of us offered our feeble applause.

What did it *mean*? Beats me. All I know is that God was there, in the flesh, and that no one who saw it will ever forget it. "Blessed are those who mourn, for they shall be comforted." The assignment was to bring the words to life. Now they will never lie quietly on the page for me again, because five women gave their lives to the words. They took them all the way to the edge of what they knew to do. Then the Divine Spirit took them further and everything was made new: the women, the watchers, and the words.

Do we dismiss the body's wisdom because it does not use words? The practice of wearing skin is so obvious that almost no one engages it as spiritual practice, yet here is a place to begin: with tears, aches, moans, gooseflesh, heat. The body knows—not just the individual body, but the cathedral we make when we bend our bodies together over one as good as dead. Doing that, we act out the one thing we know for sure: it is God's will that these bones live.

4

The Practice of Walking on the Earth

GROUNDEDNESS

The miracle is not to walk on water but on the earth.
—*Thich Nhat Hanh*

A couple of years ago my husband, Ed, and I spent a week at a lovely old church camp in North Carolina, complete with the requisite lake, boathouse, clay tennis courts, and rough wooden cabins. We were there for a conference with Archbishop Desmond Tutu, who endeared himself to everyone by showing up in an African dashiki, baggy running shorts, and plastic flip-flops the color of rainbow sherbet.

After his first presentation on the evening we all arrived, people streamed from the lecture hall in waves, some of them headed to bed early with a good mystery and others to gather on the porches of their cabins with bottles of spirits brought from home. Ed and I decided to take a walk down toward the lake before we did anything else, but since we had not brought flashlights we knew we would not be able to go very far.

There was most of a moon, anyway, so while we tripped over the roots in the path we could still see enough to stay on it. The part moon spilled light on the full lake. The sound of our own breathing was louder than the sound of faraway people laughing. Even though I could not see much, I could still smell the earth waking up to spring: pine sap, lake mud, tender green things.

When we came out from under the trees at the end of the path, we were not ready to go back, so we kept walking across the dam. Before we knew it, we were standing at the mouth of the path on the other side. I say "mouth" because the path leads through a tunnel of Carolina laurel, starting with a portal that showed up that night as a dark round "O" in the moonlight.

"Want to try it?" Ed said.

"It's dark," I said.

"It sure is," Ed said.

"Let's try it," I said.

Inside the tunnel, neither of us could see our feet, much less the way ahead, but we knew the path and we knew each other, so we slowed down and shifted into a gear that I had never used before. Without sight, I relied first of all on sound, realizing within a couple of steps that I could *hear* when I got closer to the branches on either side of me. The sound of my breath had less room to bounce around in. I could hear how the laurels muffled it on one side or the other as I drew nearer them, which was my cue to move back toward the center of the path.

More than that, I could *feel* the presence of the laurels, the same way I could feel the presence of Ed. I have heard this described as a sixth sense—the ability to align the body in space—which comes in handy when you are trying to walk through a doorway or park the car in a garage. I did not know that it worked even without sight, but it did that night. When I strayed too far to the left or to the right, I could feel the laurels practically breathing on my face, and when I did I found my way back to the center of the path again.

Pretty soon Ed and I were walking by faith and not by sight. The faith was not in an unseen deity, however. It was faith in this exquisite physical fine-tuning that neither of us had known we had, which allowed us to find our way in the dark without flashlights. After a while we got so good at it that we invented an advanced level of the game, shutting our eyes and taking turns leading without touching each other.

First Ed led, leaving me to find the almost palpable cord that connected us. It reminded me of what happened years ago when our knees were still good enough to go running together. If I could draw near enough to him when I was tired, running just off to the side behind one of his shoulders, then I could hook on to him without touching him, letting him pull me along until I could catch a second wind.

The same thing happened on the path in the dark, only I was moving much more slowly and I was not tired, so the connection felt more like a belay line than a tow truck. By focusing on Ed's presence ahead of me and trusting the unseen connection between us, I could walk much more confidently in the dark than I could when I took the lead. When it was my turn up front, I went back to my newfound navigational skills, which I exercised all the more carefully because I knew Ed was depending on me.

When we finally reached the road at the end of the lake walk, the familiar landmark took me by surprise. I had lost all sense of time on my walk through the dark tunnel. As we approached the lights of the lodge once again, I would not have been surprised to discover that we had been gone a hundred years, nor to find people still streaming from the lecture hall as if we had never left.

Not everyone is able to walk, but most people can, which makes walking one of the most easily available spiritual practices of all. All it takes is the decision to walk with some awareness, both of who you are and what you are doing. Where you are going is not as important, however counterintuitive that may seem. To detach the walking from the destination is in fact one of the best ways to recognize the altars you are passing right by all the time. Most of us spend so much time thinking about where we have been or where we are supposed to be going that we have a hard time recognizing where we actually are. When someone asks us where we want to be in our lives, the last thing that occurs to us is to look down at our feet and say, "Here, I guess, since this is where I am."

This truth is borne out by the labyrinth—an ancient spiritual practice that is enjoying a renaissance in the present century. For those who have never seen one, a labyrinth is a kind of maze. Laid out in a perfect circle with a curling path inside, it rarely comes with walls. Instead, it trusts those who enter it to stay on the path voluntarily. This path may be outlined with hand-placed stones out-of-doors or painted right on the floor indoors. Either way, it includes switchbacks and detours, just like life. It has one entrance, and it leads to one center.

The important thing to note is that the path goes nowhere. You can spend an hour on it and end up twelve feet from where you began. The journey is the point. The walking is the thing.

Not too long ago I walked a labyrinth for the first time in my life. I had flirted with labyrinths for years, but my expectations were so high that I kept finding reasons not to walk one. I did not want to hurry. I did not want to share the labyrinth with anyone who might distract me. I did not want to be disappointed. I looked forward to walking a labyrinth so much that looking forward to it kept me from doing it for years.

Then one day I met a woman who showed me the labyrinth on her land. Set in a small grove of pines, it was made of found stones, with a large one as round as a pillow near the entrance. When the wind blew, invisible chimes tinkled in the branches overhead, while pine needles sifted down to pad the circular path below. Beyond the edge of the trees I saw a small pond sparkling in the sun, and two horses grazing behind a fence. I could walk the labyrinth whenever I wanted to, my host said, even if she were not there. I did not even have to call first.

With all of my excuses gone, I returned one late summer afternoon, said a prayer, and entered the labyrinth. The first thing I noticed was that I resented following a set path. Where was the creativity in that? Why couldn't there be more than one way to go? The second thing I noticed was how much I wanted to step over the stones when they did not take me directly to the center. Who had time for all those switchbacks, with the destination so clearly in sight? The third thing I noticed was that reaching the center was no big deal. The view from there was essentially the same as the view from the start. My only prize was the heightened awareness of my own tiresome predictability.

I thought about calling it a day and going over to pat the horses, but since I predictably follow the rules even while grousing about them, I turned around to find my way out of the labyrinth again. Since I had already been to the center, I was not focused on getting there anymore. Instead, I breathed in as much of the pine smell as I could, sucking in the smell of sun and warm stones along with it. When I breathed out again, I noticed how

soft the pine needles were beneath my feet. I saw the small me-
mentos left by those who had preceded me on the path: a cement
frog, a rusted horseshoe, a stone freckled with shiny mica. I noticed how much more I notice when I am not preoccupied with
getting somewhere.

When the path delivered me back to where I had begun, I lay
down with my head on the stone pillow and dreamed the same
dream Jacob dreamed, the night he saw the angels of God climbing up and down a ladder right where he lay. *Surely the Lord is in
this place—and I did not know it!*

The beauty of physical practices like this one is that you do
not have to know what you are doing in order to begin. You just
begin, and the doing teaches you what you need to know. What
do you need to know? How would I know? When I walked that
labyrinth in the pines, I walked it in my 5'10" white woman's
body—a body with a history that is not identical, as far as I know,
to anyone else's. I walked it with my own particular compulsivity,
which gave me a chance to notice my own distinct anxieties and
longings. If I had walked it on a Tuesday instead of a Saturday,
I might have had a different experience. If I had walked it with
someone else instead of alone, I certainly would have walked it
differently. With so many variables available to me all by myself,
I cannot imagine the possibilities available to those who walk the
path wearing their own skin. The labyrinth may be a set path,
but it does not offer a set experience. Instead, it offers a door
that anyone may go through, to discover realities that meet each
person where each most needs to be met.

I suppose this is frustrating to people who want spiritual practices to work the same way a treadmill does. I have a treadmill,
which works very well. If I follow the instructions, walking at
least thirty minutes every day to elevate my heart rate up to (but

not more than) 130 beats per minute, then I can expect certain predictable results. Over time, I can lower my pulse, improve my muscle tone, and maybe even lose a little weight. My treadmill is no respecter of persons. It delivers reliable results to anyone who uses it on a regular basis. It makes promises it can keep, at least to those who use it the way they are supposed to.

Spiritual practices are not like this. The only promise they make is to teach those who engage in them what those practitioners need to know—about being human, about being human with other people, about being human in creation, about being human before God. The great religious traditions of the world are so confident of this that they commend dozens of spiritual practices to their followers without telling those practitioners exactly what will happen when they do. "Go to your cell," advised the Desert Fathers of the fourth century, "and your cell will teach you everything." If you want more details than that, the only way to get them is to choose a practice and begin.

Once, when a friend of mine wanted me to show him how to ride a horse, he kept asking me questions before he would get on. He wanted me to tell him all about the saddle, the bridle, the reins, the age of the horse, the direction of the path, the height of the branches he might encounter, the location of the "eject" button on the saddle.

"Get on," I said, while the horse stamped her foot.

"What?" my friend said, the whites of his eyes showing.

"Just get on," I said, bending over to make a step out of my hands. So he did, and twenty minutes later he was sounding like a cowboy mystic.

"This is fantastic," he said. "I am *one* with this horse." Things like that can happen when you give your mind a time-out so your body can embark on the journey.

. . .

As I said earlier, not everyone is able to walk. Thich Nhat Hanh is a Vietnamese Buddhist monk who has figured out a way around that reality. At Plum Village, his monastic community in southern France, he teaches many forms of attentiveness, including walking meditation. To watch a Buddhist monk practice walking meditation is like watching a lunar eclipse. First the bare heel extends over the earth, coming down so slowly that not even a dry leaf is displaced. Then the arch begins its long descent, laying itself down like a cat. Finally the toes arrive, beginning with the small one and ending with the big. Imperceptibly, the arrival turns into a departure as one heel rises and the other comes down.

Up above, the monk shows no signs of having made any of this happen. His face is as still as the moon. This is no circus performer on a high wire. This is a man walking on the earth. The only thing that sets him apart from any other walker is his full devotion to what he is doing. He chops carrots the same way. He hauls water the same way. Whatever he does, he does it with a groundedness that his watchers can only envy.

When someone comes to Plum Village in a wheelchair, an instructor finds a comfortable place for that person to sit and watch the walkers. He asks her to pick one of the walkers, focusing intently on what that person is doing as she deepens her own breathing. Watch the movement, he tells her. Notice the exact moment each foot leaves the ground. See the shape of the arc the foot makes as it finds its way back down. When your mind wanders, ride your breath back to the present moment. After about twenty minutes of this, most people discover at least two things: first, that they can do walking meditation without leaving their chairs; and second, that their bodies are not as localized as they had thought. Watching the walkers, they sometimes lose track of whose foot is in the air.

A few years ago a friend of mine was walking the Mother Labyrinth in Chartres Cathedral with a group of other pilgrims when she noticed an older man and woman standing near the entrance watching. After about twenty minutes of looking, they walked straight to the center of the labyrinth and bowed their heads in prayer. Then the woman took off her shoes and handed them to her husband, along with her purse. As he watched, she took the long way out of the labyrinth, following the path this time. She cried on the way. He cried just watching her. When they had pulled themselves together, my friend went up to ask them what had just happened.

They had come to celebrate the end of the woman's treatment for breast cancer, they explained. They had never even heard of a labyrinth before they walked into the cathedral that day. The woman could not explain why she was drawn to walk it, but when she did her husband decided to hold down the center, giving thanks for her life while she found her way out.

"I began to feel at peace in my body again after being very angry that it had let me down," the woman explained. Walking, she found herself remembering all the people who had walked with her through her surgery and treatment. "I now know this is why we came here," she told my friend.[2]

Solviture ambulando, wrote Augustine of Hippo, one of the early theologians of the Christian church. "It is solved by walking." What is "it"? If you want to find out, then you will have to do your own walking.

• • •

SOMETIMES WE DO NOT KNOW what we know until it comes to us through the soles of our feet, the embrace of a tender lover, or the kindness of a stranger. Touching the truth with our minds alone is not enough. We are made to touch it with our bodies. I think this is why Christian tradition clings to the reality of resurrection, even when no one can explain it to anyone else's satisfaction. The immortality of the soul is much easier to conceive than the resurrection of the body. *What? You mean a stopped heart suddenly starts again? You mean a dead body gets up with a growling stomach?* No, I mean God loves bodies. I mean that in some way that defies all understanding, God means to welcome risen bodies and not just disembodied souls to heaven's banquet table. The resurrection of the dead is the radical insistence that matter matters to God.

Still, there is no sense spending much time on that when most people do not even know how to walk. I have watched people walk, so I know. People walk with cell phones pressed to their ears, so that they cannot hear the mockingbird doing imitations of a postal truck backing up. Some people walk in pointed shoes so painful that they wince with every step, while others wear shoes so padded out with cushions, lights, and retractable wheels that they are walking on their shoes, not the earth.

Among the hardest walkers for me to watch are small children being hauled along by their wrists. Parents tell me that this is sometimes necessary, but since I have never been a parent I would not know. I do know that most of the adults doing the hauling do not mean to be unkind. They are simply used to walking, while the child is not. The child has only recently learned how to walk, so she still knows how. She feels the heat radiating up from the sidewalk. She hears the tapping of her shoes on the cement. She sees the dime someone has dropped in the crosswalk, which she leans toward before being yanked upright again. The child is so exposed to the earth that even an acorn underfoot would topple her, which may be why her adult is hanging on so tightly. But the speed is too much for her. Her arm is stretched so far it hurts. She has to run where her adult walks, and if that adult is talking on a cell phone, then really, she might be better off in jail.

The spiritual practice of walking has a long history in the world's great wisdom traditions. One of the Five Pillars of Islam is the hajj, or pilgrimage to Mecca, undertaken during the twelfth month of the lunar year. Dressed only in a white cloth that many will use later for their shrouds, pilgrims walk seven times around the ancient Ka'ba in the center courtyard of the Great Mosque. They walk counterclockwise, against the march of time, scraping away the crusted sins that have accumulated during all that time. The oldest among them would be happy to die before they are through, returning to God as clean as the day they were born.

Since the Great Mosque cannot accommodate all the Muslims in the world during a single month, pilgrims circle the Ka'ba all through the year. On any given night, thousands of them make the sacred walk around the center of their universe, in which direction they have prayed five times a day for as long as they can remember. From high in the air, they look like a small galaxy, with thousands of bits of stardust circling a square black sun.

While Jerusalem is Islam's third holiest city, for Jews and Christians it is number one. Even in troubled times the Old City flows with pilgrims, each headed to his or her own holy place. When I was there years ago, I visited the Church of the Holy Sepulcher almost daily for a month without ever entering the tiny tomb itself. My decision was not rational. Every time I drew near, I was repelled, as if some guardian angel were protecting me from the spiritual explosion that awaited me inside. So I walked around the sepulcher instead, visiting the Coptic priest who sat in the tiny chapel attached to the back of the tomb. I sat on a stone bench near the entrance, where I could watch other people enter and exit the tomb apparently unscathed.

One afternoon I watched a group of Asian tourists make videos of one another emerging from the tomb with wide grins on their faces. Another afternoon I watched a group of teenagers in matching T-shirts go in and out one by one, while their adult adviser stood like a Roman sentry at the door. Since the Church of the Holy Sepulcher is the last stop on the Via Dolorosa—the path Jesus may have walked on his way from Pilate's headquarters to Golgotha—it is not unusual to see a group of Christians approaching the church behind someone carrying a rough wooden cross. Even those who do not want to suffer what he suffered still want to walk where he walked.

In other parts of the world, Buddhist pilgrims perform full prostrations as they make their sacred journeys to Bodh Gaya in India or Mount Kailash in Tibet. I do not mean one full prostration every hour or so. I mean one full prostration after another, so that they spend more time flat on their bellies than they do standing on their feet. In other parts of the world, there are still a few Christian pilgrims who approach sacred sites on their knees.

While it is possible to construe this as what was once called "mortification of the flesh," I think it is more than that. You can walk somewhere without thinking, after all. You can mean to walk to the post office and end up at the drugstore instead. You can walk the dog without ever noticing the old woman sitting by the open window of her fifth-floor apartment, or the first reddening of dogwood leaves in the fall. You can run four miles without hearing anything but the recorded soundtrack you have chosen for the occasion.

If you get down on your knees, however, you are likely to become exquisitely aware of what you are doing. You will not miss much on your knees. Every seed-sized piece of gravel will announce itself to you. Every pound you weigh will impress itself on you. You will miss even less on your belly. Have you ever had a chance to smell the earth across which you are moving? Up close, I mean. Have you ever had a chance to feel the difference between dirt cooled by shade and heated by sun through the palms of your hands? Once, when I lay down to rest on a walk in the high Andes, I ended up with half of my body in the frost under a still-frozen bush while the other half roasted in the sun.

The body is a great focuser, whether the means is pain or pleasure. The body is a great reminder of where we came from and where we are going, on the one sacred journey that we all make whether we mean to or not.

Jesus walked a lot, and not only during the last week of his life. The four gospels are peppered with accounts of him walking into the countryside, walking by the Sea of Galilee, walking in the Temple, and even walking on water. If Jesus had driven a car instead, it is difficult to imagine how that might have changed his impact. Surely someone could have loaned him a fast horse. Instead, he walked everywhere he went, except for a short stint on a donkey at the end. This gave him time to see things, like the milky eyes of the beggar sitting by the side of the road, or the round black eyes of sparrows sitting in their cages at the market.

If he had been moving more quickly—even to reach more people—these things might have become a blur to him. Because he was moving slowly, they came into focus for him, just as he came into focus for them. Sometimes he had a destination and sometimes he did not. For many who followed him around, he *was* the destination. Whether he was going somewhere or nowhere at all, going with him was the point. Food tasted better at the pace he set. Stories lasted longer. Talk went deeper. While many of his present-day admirers pay close attention to what he said and did, they pay less attention to the pace at which he did it. Jesus was a walker, not a rider. He took his sweet time.

Those who wish to follow him more nearly might decide to take more of theirs too. A journey to Jerusalem is one way to follow his footsteps. So is walking anywhere, even around the backyard. While I am sure someone else has already thought of it, I would like to introduce the spiritual practice of going barefoot. This practice requires no props. You do not even have to be religious to do it, but if you are, then here is the scriptural warrant for it: "Remove the sandals from your feet, for the place on which you are standing is holy ground."³ That is what the Almighty said to Moses after Moses turned aside from tending sheep to investigate a blazing bush that was not burned up.

If you have visited Saint Catherine's monastery in the Sinai, then you have likely paid a visit to the legendary descendant of that bush. When I went, I was asked to remove my sandals before I entered the Chapel of the Burning Bush. Before I could even focus on the spindly bush growing against one wall of the chapel, I had to look down at my feet, which were disappearing into the gaudiest red plush carpet I had ever seen. Since the bush was no longer on fire, I guess the monks thought a fiery-looking carpet was the next best thing.

But you do not need to go to the Sinai desert to engage the practice of going barefoot. Just choose a place outdoors that you are willing to encounter in the flesh without your customary cushion and protection—a mossy knoll, if you are a beginner, or a rocky streambed, if you are not. Take off your shoes and feel the earth under your feet, as if the ground on which you are standing really is holy ground. Let it please you. Let it hurt you a little. Feel how the world really feels when you do not strap little tanks on your feet to shield you from the way things really are.

It will help if you do not expect God to speak to you. Just give your full attention to where you are, for once. Walk as if your life depended on it, placing your heel before your toes and getting a sense of just how much pressure you put on the grass, the clover—watch out for the honeybee!—the slick river stones, the silted streambed, the red clay, the pine bark on the woodland path, the black earth of the vegetable garden. As you press down on these things, can you feel them pressing back? They have been around so much longer than you have, most of them. *You* are the new kid on the block.

You might even walk in a small circle, so that you have a chance to see the same things over and over again, seeing something different in them each time. The last time you walked by the day lily, a drop of dew was hanging from one orange petal, shining like a small sun. This time it is gone, thanks to a small breeze that is cooling your upper lip. "Consider the lilies of the field," Jesus said, but you do not consider them, not usually, or at least not like this. What else have you missed in your rush from here to there?

You may have to handle your anxiety about being seen walking in circles with no shoes on, but even that can be revelatory. Why are you so afraid of what people may think about you? Since when did looking good become your god? If you like, you may take your mind off this by giving a thought to people who go barefoot because they have no shoes. What would it be like to walk through the world with so little cushion? What might your feet look like if you hunted for your lunch in a garbage dump?

Done properly, the spiritual practice of going barefoot can take you halfway around the world and wake you up to your own place in the world all at the same time. It can lead you to love God with your whole self, and your neighbor as yourself, without leaving your backyard. Just do it, and the doing will teach you what you need to live. Or keep your shoes on, if you wish. As long as you are on the earth and you know it, you are where you are supposed to be. You have everything you need to ground yourself in God.

5

The Practice of Getting Lost

WILDERNESS

Why, when God's world is so big,
did you fall asleep in a prison
of all places?

—*Jelaluddin Rumi*

When I first moved to the land where I live, I shared it with a herd of cows. The first thing I noticed about them was that they were pure white. The second thing I noticed was how predictable they were. With a hundred acres at their disposal, they had worn narrow paths across those acres to their favorite watering holes, shady spots, and clover patches. When they wanted to get from one of those places to another, they lined up single file and followed the tracks they had made across vast expanses of pasture. Some of these tracks were no more than eight inches wide, which is about one-fourth the width of a cow. Yet the cows knew exactly where to put their feet, even without looking.

Since I soon found myself following those same tracks when I walked the land, I think I understand something about why the cows use them. In most cases, the tracks mark the shortest route from point A to point B. Where they do not, that is because the cows have found ways to get where they are going without expending too many calories. In these cases, the tracks avoid both steep climbs and dicey descents, choosing long stretches under leafy tree lines wherever possible.

For my purposes, the most valuable thing about the tracks is that I can see where I am putting my feet. This is important when you share land with timber rattlers and groundhogs as well as white cows. The last thing you want when you are half a mile from home is to surprise a sunbathing rattlesnake or step into a groundhog burrow, which can swallow your leg up to the knee-cap before you even see it. Did I mention the yellow jackets? They too make homes in the deep grass, and they value their privacy.

So I understand the use of narrow paths through wide swaths of unpredictable territory. I do the same thing when I drive to work, taking the shortest route with the lightest traffic, even when that means I see the same subdevelopments and strip malls every day. I take this track so unconsciously that on the days when I mean to deviate from it—to run an errand or to keep an appointment in another direction—I sometimes find myself a mile past my unusual turn before I come to my senses.

I am convinced that this is normal human behavior, which means that something extra is needed to override it. Why override it? Because once you leave the cow path, the unpredictable territory is full of life. True, you cannot always see where you are putting your feet. This means you can no longer afford to stay unconscious. You can no longer count on the beat-down red dirt path making all of your choices for you. Leaving it, you agree to make your own choices for a spell. You agree to become aware of each step you take, tuning all of your senses to exactly where you are and exactly what you are doing.

When I do this, I hear the buzzing of the yellow jackets in time to take a detour around their front door. I see the gap in the grass around the groundhog hole in time to step around it. I sing old Baptist hymns to warn the snakes that I am coming. They do not want to see me any more than I want to see them, after all. What I see instead is the tiny wild blue iris that grows close the ground. I see the round bed in the tall grass where the doe sleeps with her twin fawns at night, and the hornet's nest no bigger than a fist, hanging from the underside of a thistle leaf.

Leaving the known path turns out to be such a boon to my senses—such a remedy for my deadening habit of taking the safest, shortest route to wherever I am (usually late) going—that I decide to get lost on my way home from work. I turn left down a road I have never followed before, though I have lived a dozen years in this small county. The road leads me into the ghost town of an old mill on the river, where the hulks of deserted buildings perch at the edge of the river like a herd of petrified mastodons. Turning away from them, I follow the winding road past an old softball diamond, complete with ramshackle bleachers, where the mill workers must have played at one time.

Before I know it, I am lost in the lives of those people as well—living in mill houses, going to the mill church, working for mill owners who paid them in chits they could use at the mill store—which, like the softball diamond, has fallen into ruin. But the road I have chosen to get lost on will not let me stay there. Leading me past the boundaries of the old mill town, it turns to dirt, taking me through a stretch of woods before presenting me with a small neighborhood of consummate country houses. One house has been added on to so often that it looks like a dowager who has had too much cosmetic surgery. Another has so many whirligigs in the yard that I do not register the house at all. A third sits at an unfortunate bend in the road, so that the porch, the windows, and the once-white siding are all covered with fine red dust churned up by passing motorists. A hand-painted sign in the front yard reads, "Slow Please."

By the time this unknown road dumps me back onto a highway I know, my detour has cost me ten minutes—a fortune, at the fevered pitch of my day—which I gladly pay for the liberating proof that I am still able to leave the thin paths I have worn with my frugal, fearful hooves.

THESE ARE BENIGN FORMS of getting lost, I know, but you have to start somewhere. If you do not start choosing to get lost in some fairly low-risk ways, then how will you ever manage when one of life's big winds knocks you clean off your course? I am not speaking literally here, although literal lostness is a good place to begin since the skills are the same: managing your panic, marshalling your resources, taking a good look around to see where you are and what this unexpected development might have to offer you.

In my life, I have lost my way more times than I can count. I have set out to be married and ended up divorced. I have set out to be healthy and ended up sick. I have set out to live in New England and ended up in Georgia. When I was thirty, I set out to be a parish priest, planning to spend the rest of my life caring for souls in any congregation that would have me. Almost thirty years later, I teach school. The last time I tried to iron one of my old black cotton clergy shirts, the rotted fabric gave way beneath my fingers.

While none of these displacements was pleasant at first, I would not give a single one of them back. I have found things while I was lost that I might never have discovered if I had stayed on the path. I have lived through parts of life that no one in her right mind would ever willingly have chosen, finding enough overlooked treasure in them to outweigh my projected wages in the life I had planned. These are just a few of the reasons that I have decided to stop fighting the prospect of getting lost and engage it as a spiritual practice instead. The Bible is a great help to me in this practice, since it reminds me that God does some of God's best work with people who are truly, seriously lost.

Take Abraham and Sarah, for instance, the first parents of the Hebrew people. The Bible gives no reason for God's choice of Abraham and Sarah except their willingness to get lost. They were not young. They were not spiritual giants. All they really had going for them was their willingness to set off on a divinely inspired trip without a map, equipped with nothing but God's promise to be with them. Most Sunday school teachers stop there, but if you follow Abraham and Sarah all the way to Egypt and back, you get the kinds of details that mark genuine wilderness time. Abraham passed Sarah off as his sister at least twice to avoid getting hurt by powerful men who found her attractive. Abraham had terrible dreams in which God showed him the suffering that would come upon his descendants. Sarah got so tired of Abraham asking her if she was pregnant yet that she sent him in to sleep with her hand-maid Hagar. By the time Sarah had her own baby, Hagar's son was big enough to pose a threat. So Sarah banished Hagar and her boy from the camp, sending them into the desert to die—but that is another wilderness story, to be saved for another time.

Ostensibly none of this would have happened if Abraham and Sarah had just thanked God for the interesting travel suggestion and said no, they thought they would just stay home in Ur where they belonged. By saying yes instead—by consenting to get lost—they selected a family gene that would become dominant in years to come.

Long after Abraham and Sarah's bones had turned to dust, their descendants ended up in Egypt again. The cow paths they followed in that land led straight from their slave huts to the mud pits where they made bricks. They always knew where their next meal was coming from. They never had to wonder what they were going to do in the morning. The cost of such security was their bondage to Pharaoh, who was happy with their labor but not with their birthrate. When Pharaoh started ordering midwives to kill Hebrew baby boys, God's ears rang with the wailing outcry of the people. They cried and cried until God chose a fugitive named Moses—who had narrowly escaped being one of those dead babies himself—to lead the people out of Egypt.

The people were so happy to leave that they did not ask for any details. As it turned out, they needed forty years in the wilderness to learn the holy art of being lost. They faced not just snakes but also hunger, thirst, and terrible homesickness. Did I mention the wrath of God? There was also that, when they complained bitterly that they would trade their sacred lostness in a red-hot minute for a cow path straight back to Egypt. They did not get it, thank God. Instead, they got food dropped straight from heaven in the wilderness. They got snakebites. They got fresh water that sprang from rocks. They got whacked when they decided a golden calf was a safer bet for getting them back on track again than the God who sometimes seemed intent on destroying them. But God did not destroy them. Instead, God strengthened that wilderness gene in them, the one that made them strong and resourceful even as it reminded them how perishable they were. By the time they arrived in the land of milk and honey, they knew how to say thank you and mean it.

Follow the story with an eye for getting lost and you see how the theme sustains the plot. The prophet Elijah gets lost in the desert while fleeing the fury of a queen named Jezebel, which is how he comes to hear the voice of God in the sound of sheer silence. The people spend decades in exile in Babylon—a cultural wilderness they might never have survived without their practice in the literal wilderness of Sinai. Much later, Jesus of Nazareth consents to becoming lost, to spending forty days in the Judean desert being tested by everything from wild animals to a scripture-quoting Satan.

These are big stories, but all you really need is a flat tire to find yourself thrust suddenly into the wilderness. This has happened to me, so I know. One moment everything is fine. You are on your way home from Atlanta after a satisfying day in town. The stars are out. "Thistle and Shamrock" is on the radio. Then you hear an increasingly loud noise coming from the direction of your right front fender, while your car begins to list seriously in that same direction. By the time you wrestle the car to the shoulder of the highway, you know you have a flat tire.

Depending on your personality, the panic can begin immediately or you can hold it off for a while, opening the glove compartment to find the chapter on changing tires in the owner's manual. If you are a man, you do not look forward to this. If you are a woman alone on the road at night, your mind starts working overtime. Even if you call AAA, it might be an hour before they arrive. In the meantime there is no telling who will pull over, either to help you or to hurt you. You know you are supposed to stay in the car with the doors locked, but since your compact sways violently every time a semi whizzes by, this does not seem like the best idea.

You are truly, seriously lost, even though you know exactly where you are.

I hope you do not get hurt the same way you hope you do not get hurt. I want you back on the road as soon as possible, asleep in your bed by midnight at the latest. You may not be able to think about it until then, but something is happening to you in this wilderness that does not happen when you are safe at home. Some of it is purely physical. Because you are in danger, all the blood in your body has raced toward your heart, abandoning your hands and feet to an icy tingling. Your senses are on full alert. You can smell engine oil and spent rubber along with your own sweat. You can see the glow in the sky away up ahead, showing you where the next highway exit is. You can hear your heart pounding in the empty closet of your chest.

Even though you would rather not think about it, you are exquisitely vulnerable in this moment. You are vulnerable *to* this moment. Your carefully maintained safety net has ripped. Your expensive armor has sprung a leak. You are in need of help, and your awareness of this is not a bad thing. If hauling water brings you into communion with people you have never met, then so does sitting in this wilderness. There are people all over the world who know how helpless you are feeling right now. Plenty of them would trade places with you in a minute, to be sitting in a wilderness where there are no bombs going off, no guns being fired. If you listen to these people, they may be able to convince you that the odds of your survival are very, very good.

Even if the odds were against you, there is something holy in this moment of knowing just how perishable you are. It is part of the truth about what it means to be human, however hard most of us work not to know that. Five years ago, before my father died, he filled a glass carafe with water. It sits in the room where he read books in a bentwood rocker, stopping from time to time to pour himself a glass of water. Five years later, the glass carafe and the water are still there, although my father is not.

As unreasonable as this seems to me—that blown glass and poured water should last longer than my father's flesh—I do not look at that carafe without being mindful that life evaporates more easily than water. I do not look at it without being swamped with love for my father, as well as with gratitude for my next liquid breath. Faced with the solid reality of such loss, I know how to say thank you and mean it.

IN CHRISTIAN TRADITION, one of the most solemn days of the church year is Ash Wednesday, when believers enter a season of preparation for Easter by confronting their own mortality. That this season lasts forty days is no mistake. Those who follow Jesus are meant to follow him into the wilderness, where they too may be tested.

For me, at least, the peak of the service comes when the priest invites the congregation forward to the altar rail to receive ashes on our foreheads. Those of us who have done it before know that we are being invited to our own funerals. Kneeling shoulder to shoulder at the rail, we wait our turn, hearing the priest say to others what will soon be said to us. "Remember that you are dust, and to dust you shall return," the priest says to me, making the sign of the cross on my forehead.

Because she has just dipped her thumb in the cup of ashes, I get the full dose. Extra ashes fall on the bridge of my nose. I worry for a moment about how silly I will look when I stand up and turn around. Then I get the sudden urge to ask for more, to ask for a whole bowl of ashes on my head. But it is not yet my turn for a whole bowl. For now, all I get is a taste of death, while there is still time to say please and thank you to the Giver of all life.

Popular religion focuses so hard on spiritual success that most of us do not know the first thing about the spiritual fruits of failure. When we fall ill, lose our jobs, wreck our marriages, or alienate our children, most of us are left alone to pick up the pieces. Even those of us who are ministered to by brave friends can find it hard to shake the shame of getting lost in our lives. And yet if someone asked us to pinpoint the times in our lives that changed us for the better, a lot of those times would be wilderness times.

When the safety net has split, when the resources are gone, when the way ahead is not clear, the sudden exposure can be both frightening and revealing. We spend so much of our time protecting ourselves from this exposure that a weird kind of relief can result when we fail. To lie flat on the ground with the breath knocked out of you is to find a solid resting place. This is as low as you can go. You told yourself you would die if it ever came to this, but here you are. You cannot help yourself and yet you live.

A couple of years ago I ran into a tree while I was riding a horse. At least I think I ran into a tree. All I remember is rising in my saddle to take a jump between two trees. Then I remember waking briefly with a saddle under my head, hearing a siren, and waking again in the hospital. When a nurse saw me open my eyes, she asked me whom she should call. Although my head hurt so badly that even thinking about her question hurt, I recalled that my husband was out of town. So were my parents. "I can't think," I said, and passed out.

When I woke again, I reached up to feel the stitches in the back of my head. When I pulled my hand away, a sticky spider web came with it. I patted my head and felt twigs in my hair. I remembered I had sisters, whose names I gave the nurse. A friend showed up, who told me nothing was broken. She also explained the twigs. I had a concussion, she said, which made washing my head a bad idea. I could get clean later. At the moment my job was to lie still.

I did my job well for the next several days, learning to use a bedpan because I could not balance well enough to stand upright. When I fell asleep, I fell into nightmares so vivid that I fought to stay awake. When I was awake, I struggled to use a brain that did not work the way it used to. I felt as if I had suffered the sudden onset of senile dementia. I could not remember words. To complete a thought took ages, to complete a sentence even longer. When someone came to see me, I had to swim my way up out of murky depths to focus on a face or recall a name.

The first miracle of this time was that people took care of me when I could not care for myself. When I was knocked out cold, someone called an ambulance for me. Someone stitched my head. When no member of my family knew where I was, a stranger brought me food. Since I have made a point all my life of being the one who brings the food, not the one who needs it, this reversal did wonders for me. To receive the hospitality of strangers changed me far more than providing it ever did.

The second miracle was how safe I felt, although not in any conventional sense. My head hurt like hell. I had such depraved dreams that I could not imagine where the vile images in them had come from. Wild dogs ate babies, while skeletons rattled their loose bones at me. Had the concussion opened a sewer line in my head? Was a demon messing with me? In the grip of those nightmares I feared I might die, or at least never return to who I had once been. Yet as badly as I was frightened, I was also held. The safety I felt was located far beyond my pain and fear. When I closed my eyes I could almost see it—beyond the foot of my bed, beyond the wall of my hospital room—a second net that I could see through the ripped strands of the first, one I knew would catch me no matter how far I fell. Although my injuries were human, my safety felt divine.

Since I know plenty of people who have been hurt badly, both physically and otherwise, without sensing that same safety, I stay curious about where it comes from. Maybe it is an effect of early childhood experience. Maybe it is a denial mechanism. Maybe it is the grace of God. Whatever it is, I have no control over it. All I can do is pay attention to what happens when I am lost in the wilderness, with no ability to help myself.

At this advanced level, the practice of getting lost has nothing to do with wanting to go there. It is something that happens, like it or not. You lose your job. Your lover leaves. The baby dies. At this level, the advanced practice of getting lost consists of consenting to be lost, since you have no other choice. The consenting itself becomes your choice, as you explore the possibility that life is for you and not against you, in spite of all the evidence to the contrary.

This rock-bottom trust seems to come naturally to some people, while it takes disciplined practice for others. I am one of the latter, a damaged truster who hopes she has lots of time to work up to the advanced level before her own exodus comes. To that end, I keep my eyes open for opportunities to get slightly lost, so that I can gradually build the muscles necessary for radical trust.

Travel is easily the most pleasurable way to do this, since it is almost impossible to leave home without making a wrong turn somewhere. When I do, I stop to ask someone where I am instead of pulling over to consult my map. I know this is easier for women than it is for men. (Why does it take thousands of sperm to fertilize a single egg? Because the sperm refuse to stop and ask for directions.) I also know plenty of women who hate to ask for help, which makes this an equal-opportunity exercise. The point is to give up on the sufficiency of your own resources. The point is to admit that you are lost, and maybe even to allow that you are in no hurry to be found.

The French have a word for this. When someone goes for a walk with no particular destination in mind, willing to go wherever the wind blows him, that person is a *flâneur*. He saunters. He strolls. He takes a right out of his apartment building one day, having taken a left yesterday. He walks until the smell of fresh bread leads him to make his first turn, down a side street with a bakery. He continues his walk with a fresh Danish in his hand, until a jogger passes him with a sleek gray dog on a leash. The jogger turns right at the next light so the *flâneur* does too, going about half a block before he finds himself in front of a stamp and coin store that has always intrigued him.

Since he is a *flâneur* he has time to go in. When he comes back out, he knows that Bhutan, of all places, is known for its postage stamps, which include Walt Disney characters as well as commemorative issues featuring the British royal family. After that, he chooses his turns based on his associations with the names of the streets, ending up on one he has walked many times before. This time, however, the window boxes in front of one house are full of freshly planted red geraniums. He knows the smell so well that he does not know whether he is really smelling them or only imagining that he is smelling them. Either way, life is good for this *flâneur*. Because he is going no place in particular, he does not miss a thing. Plus, this pleasure is affordable. So far this morning has cost him $1.49, the price of a cherry Danish.

When my husband and I married, neither of us had ever traveled outside of the United States. I planned our first trip to the Yucatan, arranging for a rental car that we would pick up and return to the airport in Merida. In between, we would explore Chichenitza and Cozumel, spending a couple of days in a quaint hotel on Isla Mujeres. It was not until we were trying to find our way out of the rental lot at the airport that we fully focused on the fact that neither of us knew Spanish.

"What do you think 'Salida' means?" I asked Ed, as we passed a sign with that word on it for the third time.

"South?" he said.

After two more times around the parking lot, we learned our first vocabulary word: *salida* means "exit" in Spanish.

We both learned to ask for directions on that trip. We paid large fines to Mexican policemen who stopped us for road violations we never understood, although they did help us understand that if we gave them money, then we would not have to go to jail. We learned important phrases such as "Dos cervezas, por favor," and "Dónde está el baño?" We swam in cenotes with blue water as clear as bathwater. We sat out a storm in front of a tortilla shop, eating piles of fresh corn tortillas with our hands while the rain pounded the roof of our rental car. We paid a fisherman to take us on a day trip to an island full of birds, where he cooked us a barracuda for lunch over a fire on the beach. He gave me the head to eat, since that was the best part.

After that trip, Ed and I started traveling with a company that planned all the details for us, including a guide who spoke the language. We have been to all kinds of places that I will never forget, but that first trip to Mexico remains the most vivid. We were lost most of the time. We met people willing to help us find our way. We saw things we could not have planned to see. I know it is a stretch to call this a spiritual practice, but perhaps that is the point. Anything can become a spiritual practice once you are willing to approach it that way—once you let it bring you to your knees and show you what is real, including who you really are, who other people are, and how near God can be when you have lost your way.

Of course for this last to be true you have to be willing to recognize God in your neighbor. Once, when I took the wrong train to the New York Botanical Gardens and ended up walking through a pretty scary neighborhood in the Bronx, a bus driver stopped and opened his doors just for me.

"I don't have the right change," I said, my eyes huge with fear.

"Get in," he said. God drove a bus in the Bronx that day.

In the first five books of the Hebrew Bible, there is a command that runs through Torah like a hymn refrain. There are many variations on it, given in very many contexts, but the basic gist of it is, "You shall love the stranger, for you were strangers in the land of Egypt." Those most likely to befriend strangers, in other words, are those who have been strangers themselves. The best way to grow empathy for those who are lost is to know what it means to be lost yourself.

SOME OF THE BRIGHTEST PEOPLE I know have never been strangers. When I first began teaching college ten years ago, I regularly met students who had never flown on airplanes because they had never left Georgia. They could still have gotten lost, of course. All they had to do was go to the Thai grocery store in Cornelia and ask someone to explain the vegetables, or visit the Spanish mass at Saint Mark's Catholic church. Both of these adventures lie within a six-mile radius of the college, although few locals undertake them.

The students are not unusual in this regard. Most of us prefer to remain on our cow paths, where we know the language and we do not need maps because we know the way by heart. Some of us even stay behind our own fences because we do not want to be mistaken for interlopers in other people's pastures. One of my students told me the story of how a Muslim man showed up at her father's farm one day asking to buy a cow. Since her father did not know the first thing about Islam, he did not know that Muslims keep kosher, much like Jews. The Muslim word is *hallal*, but the principle is the same. The slaughter of the animal must be quick and humane. It needs to be done in a certain way, and the best way to make sure that it is done that way is to do it yourself.

But the farmer did not know any of that. All he knew was that there was a whole van full of dusky-skinned people sitting in his driveway. So he excused himself for a moment, got his shotgun, and showed it to the man at his front door. "You go now and don't you ever come back," he said to the stranger. I am just guessing, but I think he did that because he had never been a stranger himself.

One of the best things students do is to go on field trips. Remember lining up to board the yellow bus to the museum? For my students, the trip may be no longer than a ride to Atlanta, where they can visit a Hindu temple or attend a live performance at the Shakespeare Tavern. Leaving their established paths, they discover neighbors they never knew they had. More important, they go as guests, not hosts, so that they are in a better position to notice the kindness of strangers.

The students who elect longer trips overseas come back changed for good. Having gotten lost in Dublin, Madrid, or Cairo, they come home both stronger at the edges and softer at the center. They begin to listen to the news. They can find the Inner Hebrides on a map. When exchange students arrive from Bosnia, Kazakhstan, or Zambia, the students who have been far from home themselves are the first to show them around. They sit with them in the dining hall, because they too have been strangers.

However you choose to do it, the practice of getting lost is both valuable and undervalued, at least by the North American culture most of us know best. In this culture, the point is to get from point A to point B as quickly as possible, even if that means you miss most of the territory, including the packed dirt under your feet. Sometimes this is because you are doing at least five other things while you are in transit, including talking on the phone, listening to the radio, drinking a mocha latte, checking your text messages, telling your dog to get back in the backseat, and checking out how good you look in your sunglasses by admiring yourself in the rearview mirror.

Once you become lost, everything but the dog and the telephone will become suddenly unimportant—the telephone because it may allow you to call someone who loves you enough to come find you, and the dog to keep you company while you wait. If you are not able to set priorities any other way, then getting lost may be the kick in the pants you have been waiting for.

You had better do it quickly, however, since the growing popularity of Global Positioning Systems may soon make getting lost impossible to do. I think I understand the appeal. Following the instructions of a disembodied voice coming from your dashboard takes less time than pulling over to ask directions or look at a map. Plus, it may be comforting to think that a big eye in the sky can see you no matter where you are, even though this will do nothing to prevent you from missing your turn or running into the car ahead of you. I know a single woman who recently purchased a system for her car, delighted to discover that she could choose both the gender and the timbre of the voice that would speak to her. She chose the honey-coated male voice to give her directions. Even though she knows her way to the grocery store at night, she sometimes uses her GPS just so she can hear him talk to her in the dark.

You will think of other ways to get lost, or to accept that you really have gotten lost through no choice of your own. It can happen anywhere, in all kinds of ways. You can get lost on your way home. You can get lost looking for love. You can get lost between jobs. You can get lost looking for God. However it happens, take heart. Others before you have found a way in the wilderness, where there are as many angels as there are wild beasts, and plenty of other lost people too. All it takes is one of them to find you. All it takes is you to find one of them. However it happens, you could do worse than to kneel down and ask a blessing, remembering how many knees have kissed this altar before you.

6

The Practice of Encountering Others

COMMUNITY

Walk joyfully on the earth and respond to that of God in every human being.

— *George Fox*

I was at least thirty years old before I learned that I am an introvert. I paid a psychologist $75 for this information and it was worth every penny. Before I learned that I was an introvert, I thought I was at least shy and possibly antisocial. At other people's parties, I stayed in the kitchen with the help. At my own parties, I was the help. When the story of Martha and Mary came up in church, no one had to tell me why Martha stayed in the kitchen while her sister Mary sat at Jesus's feet. Martha was an introvert. She found chopping potatoes far less exhausting than talking to people, and besides, she could hear everything they were saying right where she was without having to come up with something to say herself.

It can be difficult to be an introvert in church, especially if you happen to be the pastor. Liking to be alone can be interpreted as a judgment on other people's company. Liking to be quiet can be construed as aloofness. There is so much emphasis on community in most congregations that anyone who does not participate risks being labeled a loner. This is probably why I was so happy to discover the Desert Fathers, a group of early Christians whose practice of community did not include a coffee hour.

There were some Desert Mothers too, although not many. I am not sure that any of them ever called themselves by those names, but the desert was what they had in common. In the fourth century of the Common Era, just as Christianity was becoming the official religion of the Roman Empire, these pilgrims bailed out of the cities in which they lived. They had no confidence in the volatile mix of religion and politics, being pretty sure which one would rise to the top.

Taking little with them besides their wish to live as close to God as they could, they followed the example of an Egyptian monk named Anthony, who dissolved his parents' large estate six months after they left it to him. He had heard something in church about selling everything he owned and giving the proceeds to the poor, so that was what Anthony did. He gave his land away to neighboring villagers. He sold his goods and gave the money to those who needed it. Then he headed to the mountains across the Nile from his village, where he lived alone for the next twenty years.

In 305, he left the cave in which he lived to found a community of people like himself, people who lived in small cells on bare necessities, just close enough to one another to offer encouragement. One visitor to this earliest monastery said, "Their cells like tents were filled with singing, fasting, praying, and working that they might give alms, and having love and peace with one another."[1]

Anthony's desert experiment became a movement. A hundred years later, similar communities thrived not only in the deserts of Egypt but also in Palestine, Persia, and Arabia. Some were huge monasteries, populated by hundreds of monks, while others were loose confederations of desert "solitaries" who became known as the Desert Fathers. These holy hermits spent their days making baskets and seeking God, which gave them a lot of time to wrestle with their own spiritual ambitions.

"If you see a young monk by his own will climbing up into heaven," one elder said, "take him by the foot and throw him to the ground, because what he is doing is not good for him."[2] Sayings like these are all that remain of the Desert Fathers. Repeated mouth to mouth before they were finally written down in Syriac, Latin, and Greek, they survive in classical collections that have lost none of their piquancy. The Desert Fathers had tart tongues, kind hearts, and no interest in their own reputations. Whether they meant to be funny or not, they often were.

Once, two elders who were living together decided that they should have a quarrel like ordinary men. Since they had never had one before, they were not quite sure how to begin. So one of the elders looked around, found a brick, and placed it squarely between him and his brother in Christ. "I will say, 'It is mine,'" he instructed his brother. "Then you say, 'No, it is mine.' This is the sort of thing that leads to a quarrel."

"Are you ready?" he asked his brother.

"I am ready," his brother said.

"Okay," he said, regarding the brick. "It is mine."

"I beg your pardon," his brother said, "but I do believe that it is mine."

"No it's not; it's mine," the first monk said.

"Well, if it's yours, then take it," his brother said. Thus the two elders failed to get into a quarrel after all.

IF I HAD LIVED in the desert, I would not have had a roommate. Brother Arsenius was more my kind of guy. He lived thirty-two miles from his nearest neighbor in the desert of Scete. As more and more hermits arrived, they moved closer and closer to him, until Arsenius finally left there, weeping and wailing. "Worldly men have ruined Rome," he said, "and monks have ruined Scete."[3]

Yet even the monks who lived all alone came together from time to time, to celebrate communion and share a common meal afterward, over which they discussed any problems that had arisen in the community. Even if they lived thirty-two miles apart, they remained in community. They needed one another and they knew it. This was not simply a matter of physical need, although that was certainly a factor for people living in the wilderness. The deeper reason they needed one another was to save them from the temptation of believing in their own self-sufficiency.

One elder who lived all alone undertook a seventy-week fast, eating only once a week during all that time in order to become more receptive to God. When he was little more than bone and vapor, he asked God to reveal to him the meaning of a certain Bible passage, but God would not do it. The elder, disappointed by how little his fast had done for him, decided to go ask one of his brothers what the passage meant. The minute he closed the door to his cell, an angel of God appeared to him, saying, "Your seventy-week fast did not bring you one step closer to God, but now that you have humbled yourself enough to go to your brother, God sent me to reveal the meaning of the passage."[4] Then the angel told the elder what it meant and went away.

I like to think that the elder went on to visit his brother anyway, breaking his fast with him and swapping stories about what a trickster God was. At the very least, most of us need someone to tell our stories to. At a deeper level, most of us need someone to help us forget ourselves, a little or a lot. The great wisdom traditions of the world all recognize that the main impediment to living a life of meaning is being self-absorbed.

One friend of mine, who thinks quite a lot about himself, is never at a loss for words in describing his inner conflicts, his blinding insights, his small triumphs, his relapse into self-doubt, and the self-talk he uses to crawl back out of the pit again. Fortunately, he also has his own number, which is why he is a great friend. One day, as he wound down from his opening monologue, he flashed a bright smile.

"Well!" he said. "That's enough about me. What do you think about me?"

As often as I think I am seeking other people out in order to get something for myself, the deeper truth is that I am hoping they will draw me out of myself. If you have ever gotten into a conversation so compelling that you could not believe what your watch said when you looked at it, then you know what I mean. If you have ever spent a Saturday volunteering at the Special Olympics, taking Meals on Wheels to the elderly, or picking up trash with the Riverkeepers, then you know that you can arrive back home dirty and tired but also oddly refreshed, with more lift in your heart than you could have gotten from a day at the beach.

Artists and athletes speak of something called "flow." When they are deeply involved in what they are doing, time ceases to exist. So does their sense of themselves as separate from what they are doing. In the case of the artists, they become one with the paint, the chalk, the clay. In the case of the athletes, they become one with the team, the ball, the court. The body moves by instinct instead of thought. Awareness blooms, as the individual self escapes its confines to become part of something bigger than the self.

In the Christian mystical tradition, one name for this phenomenon is divine union. It can happen all alone with God, but it can also happen with other people and sometimes even with trees. It is not achieved as much as it is given—the often fleeting but fully memorable gift of escaping the small self long enough to glimpse a wholeness more real than the most real brokenness. In the light of this wholeness, it can become impossible to make meaningful distinctions between God and other people, trees, or anything else in creation. Everything that exists, exists in this wholeness. Everything that lives, lives in this light. This is the one community that matters, the one toward which all others reach.

Since spiritual people tend to like to do hard things, I know people who have traveled around the world hunting this experience of divine union. I know people who have eaten magic mushrooms, become nuns, sold all that they owned and given the proceeds to the poor. Insofar as these extreme measures have led them beyond themselves, I imagine that these people have learned a lot from them. Like the Desert Fathers, they know that if you always do what you have always done, then you will always get what you have always got. Extreme measures are sometimes called for, and these measures sometimes even produce results.

The wisdom of the Desert Fathers includes the wisdom that the hardest spiritual work in the world is to love the neighbor as the self—to encounter another human being not as someone you can use, change, fix, help, save, enroll, convince or control, but simply as someone who can spring you from the prison of yourself, if you will allow it. All you have to do is recognize another you "out there"—your other self in the world—for whom you may care as instinctively as you care for yourself. To become that person, even for a moment, is to understand what it means to die to your self. This can be as frightening as it is liberating. It may be the only real spiritual discipline there is.

For these reasons and more, the world's great religions have always required communities of people to make them work. Whether they call themselves congregations, covens, ummas, or churches, these communities are the concrete places where the teachings of the religion are tested. Sometimes the teachings explode in people's faces. Other times they save people's lives. Either way, the teachings mean little apart from the embodied practices of the community.

Abbot Pastor, one of the most often quoted Desert Fathers, once said, "If you have a chest full of clothing, and leave it for a long time, the clothing will rot inside it. It is the same with the thoughts in our heart. If we do not carry them out by physical action, after a long while they will spoil and turn bad."[5]

Of course, religious communities are not the only communities in which neighbor love is practiced. In the small rural county where I live, people also count on community theater, contra dancing, quilting circles, book clubs, singing groups, Rotary Club meetings, and even a cockfight or two to keep kinship bonds strong. The only problem with any of these groups, as far as I can tell, is that they tend to attract like-minded people, the same way most churches do. However different the people in them may be, and however often they may tangle with one another, they still share central convictions, commitments, values, or disciplines. On the one hand, this is what keeps them together. On the other hand, this is what keeps other people out.

Meanwhile, there are people in all of our communities who do not belong to any of the same groups we do. They do not live thirty-two miles away, either. Some of them live right down the street. Some of them stand right in front of us at the gas station, the post office, or the grocery store, where they remain largely invisible to us. Our community with them is human community— such a broad connection that it is easy to overlook—and yet who could be better equipped to pop the locks on our prisons than people in whom we see nothing of ourselves?

At its most basic level, the everyday practice of being with other people is the practice of loving the neighbor as the self. More intricately, it is the practice of coming face-to-face with another human being, preferably someone different enough to qualify as a capital "O" Other—and at least entertaining the possibility that this is one of the faces of God.

Like the practices of paying attention, wearing skin, walking on the earth, and getting lost, this spiritual practice requires no special setting, no personal trainer, no expensive equipment. It can be done anywhere, by anyone who resolves to do it. A good way to warm up is to focus on one of the human beings who usually sneak right past you because they are performing some mundane service such as taking your order or handing you your change. The next time you go to the grocery store, try engaging the cashier. You do not have to invite her home for lunch or anything, but take a look at her face while she is trying to find "arugula" on her laminated list of produce.

Here is someone who exists even when she is not ringing up your groceries, as hard as that may be for you to imagine. She is someone's daughter, maybe someone's mother as well. She has a home she returns to when she hangs up her apron here, a kitchen that smells of last night's supper, a bed where she occasionally lies awake at night wrestling with her own demons and angels. Do not go too far with this or you risk turning her into a character in your own novel, which is a large part of her problem already. It is enough for you to acknowledge her when she hands you your change.

"You saved eleven dollars and six cents by shopping at Winn Dixie today," she says, looking right at you. All that is required of you is to look back. Just meet her eyes for a moment when you say, "Thanks." Sometimes that is all another person needs to know that she has been seen—not the cashier but the person—but even if she does not seem to notice, the encounter has occurred. You noticed, and because you did, neither of you will ever be quite the same again.

Simple and maybe even silly as this may sound, it is such a profound practice that those who attempt it often meet with huge inner resistance. I do not *want* to encounter another human being at the cash register, thank you very much. I just want my groceries—in paper not plastic, please, as quickly as possible—so I can get on with my day, which will become interminable if I have to stop and do this tedious eye-to-eye thing with every person who crosses my path. Surely they have other people in their lives to see who they really are, to treat them as more than means to ends. I do not dispute the importance of that, I really do not, but who has the *time*? Honestly, if you knew how many things I have to get done by six o'clock tonight . . .

This is such a predictable human response that Jesus spoke directly to it, not only in the gospel of Matthew but especially there.

Then the king will say to those at his right hand, "Come, you that are blessed by my Father, inherit the kingdom prepared for you from the foundation of the world; for I was hungry and you gave me food, I was thirsty and you gave me something to drink, I was a stranger and you welcomed me, I was naked and you gave me clothing. I was sick and you took care of me, I was in prison and you visited me." Then the righteous will answer him, "Lord, when was it that we saw you . . . ?"

Matthew 25:34–37

Who has the time? In this and countless other passages, Jesus taught the practice of encounter. He taught it not only by what he said but also by what he did. He did not leave any of his clothes in a chest to rot.

Watch how this rabbi practices what he preaches and you will note that his teaching is not limited to people who look, act, or think like him. He does the same eye-to-eye thing with Roman centurions, Samaritan lepers, Syro-Phoenician women, and hostile Judeans that he does with his own Galilean disciples. He does it with slaves and rulers, twelve-year-old girls and powerful men, people who can be useful to him and people who cannot. With the possible exception of his own family, no one is dismissed from his circle of concern, for no one made in God's image is negligible in the revelation of that same God.

In biblical tradition, the practice of encounter shows up most often as the practice of hospitality, or *philoxenia*. Take the word apart and you get *philo*, from one of the four Greek words for love, and *xenia*, for stranger. Love of stranger, in other words, which is about as counterintuitive as you can get. For most of us, *xenophobia*—fear of stranger—comes much more naturally, but in that case scripture is unnatural. According to Jonathan Sacks, chief rabbi of Great Britain, "the Hebrew Bible in one verse commands, 'You shall love your neighbor as yourself,' but in no fewer than 36 places commands us to 'love the stranger.' "[6]

Why should we do that? Because we have been strangers ourselves, the Bible says. Because if we have never been strangers, then that is because we have never left home. The people of Israel did leave home, repeatedly. They knew what it was like to hear keys turning in locks and shutters being shut when they walked into a new town holding their thin children by the hand. They were used to knocking on the door of the house with the "Room for Rent" sign in the front yard and learning that the room had already been rented—always, no matter how many doors they knocked on, learning that the room had already been rented.

You shall love the stranger first of all because you know what it is to be a stranger yourself. Second of all, you shall love the stranger because the stranger shows you God. Abraham and Sarah encounter God when they welcome three strangers into their tent. Jacob encounters God when he stays up all night wrestling a stranger by the river Jabbok. When the people of Israel are in exile in Babylon, God anoints a Persian stranger named Cyrus to bring them home. In his first sermon in Luke's gospel, Jesus gets in terrible trouble for pointing out that God sent Elijah to save a widow in Sidon, and Elisha to heal a leper in Syria, when there was no shortage of widows and lepers in Israel. Why should we love the stranger? Because God does.

Hospitality became a cardinal virtue in the early church, where all Christians were "homeschooled" because there was nowhere else to go. The church was not a place but a people—also known as the household of God—who met in one another's homes and ate at one another's tables, often breaking the rules they had grown up with by eating with people who were above or below them on the human food chain.

But Jesus did not have a home he could welcome people into. He could not cook anyone a meal nor offer anyone a bed, which may be what gave him such a hospitable heart. While others opened their homes to him, lending him a table to preside over for a night, his own *philoxenia* was much more likely to take place in a field or a boat, on a road or a mountain—wherever people who felt like strangers happened to meet the person who made them feel like kin. It was a gift he had, this divine practice of encounter, so valuable to him that he did his best to teach his followers how to do it too.

It is a life-saving practice in a world where religious difference and identity have become more important than anyone could have guessed even five years ago. Turn on the news at virtually any hour and you will hear stories of conflict in which religious identity is key: blue states versus red states in the United States, Sunnis versus Shias in Iraq, Muslims versus Christians in the Sudan, Jews versus Muslims in Israel/Palestine. While I am not equipped to take on the long histories and multiple sources of all these conflicts, I know all about "versus."

I know that nothing strengthens community like a common enemy. I know that when religious people are feeling overwhelmed by a world with little use for their ancient truths, they can find new meaning by identifying a great evil to oppose. I know that the Abrahamic faiths of Judaism, Christianity, and Islam are especially vulnerable to the formation of "oppositional identity," both because the stories of their struggles with their enemies have been made sacred in their scriptures and because monotheists—one-true-God people—have never wasted much charity on those who do not acknowledge their one true God.

Here is a law as reliable as gravity: the degree to which we believe our faith is what makes us human is the same degree to which we will question the humanity of those who do not share our faith.[7]

"We have just enough religion to make us hate one another," Jonathan Swift once observed, "but not enough to make us love one another." Because we *are* human, which is to say essentially self-interested, we are always looking for ways to add a little more authority to our causes, to come up with better reasons to fight for what we want than "Because I want it, that's why." If we can convince ourselves that God wants it too—even if that means making God in our own image so we can deny the image of God in our enemies—then we are free to engage in combative piety. We are free to harm others not for our own reasons but in the name of God, which allows us to feel holy about doing it instead of just plain bad.

In his award-winning book, *Exclusion & Embrace*, Bosnian-born theologian Miroslav Volf says, "It may not be too much to claim that the future of our world will depend on how we deal with identity and difference."[8] Citizens of the United States, which is presently the most religiously diverse nation on the face of the earth, would do well to pay attention to that claim. As children of the covenant and inheritors of the gospel, we might also understand that we have the resources to do so.

WHERE ARTICLES OF BELIEF threaten to set people in opposition to one another, we may embody articles of peace.[9] Where difference is demonized, we may host suppers with surprising guest lists. Where religious identity is wedded to political power, we may resist, although never by adopting the tactics of those in charge. We may test the premise that God uses the weak to confound the strong, as well as the promise that the God who made others different from us is revealed in them as well as us. "The supreme religious challenge," says Rabbi Sacks, "is to see God's image in one who is not in our image,"[10] for only then can we see past our own reflections in the mirror to the God we did not make up.

Long before I arrived at Piedmont College, the faculty decided that Religion 101 would not be "Introduction to the Bible" or "Life of Christ" but "Religions of the World," a basic introduction to the major wisdom traditions of humankind. They decided this in spite of the fact that Piedmont is a church-related college— or, I like to think, *because* Piedmont is a church-related college. What better way for Christians to engage their commandment to love the neighbor than to learn what those neighbors hold most sacred? And while they are at it, what better way to learn more about what they hold most sacred themselves?

When I arrived in 1998, "Religions of the World" became my daily bread. I have taught it twenty times now to some five hundred students. Last year I introduced a short version of the class to students at Columbia Theological Seminary. During one memorable week last fall, thirty of us visited five centers of worship in the Atlanta area. On Friday alone, we started out with a morning communion service at the seminary, proceeded to jumma prayers at the Atlanta Masjid of al-Islam, and ended up at Congregation Or Hadash for the celebration of Simchat Torah, where some resident Jews said the sight of so many dancing Gentiles made them resolve to put more heart into their dancing too.

Afterward, our hosts invited us to their home for a sumptuous, kosher Shabbat meal. We Christians were not the ones providing hospitality this time. We were the ones receiving it, the strangers being welcomed in the name of the Lord, which turned out to be exactly what we needed. Because we belonged to the dominant religious tradition where we lived, we were used to being the ones in charge. Some of us were longtime clergy, who were used to presiding over similar meals in our own houses of worship, but we were not the officiants this time. We were the clueless guests, standing awkwardly with our hands clasped in front of us trying not to knock anything over.

There were two loaves of braided challah on the table, some candles, a bottle of Manischewitz wine, and a bowl of cotton balls beside a bowl of water. Our gentle hosts treated us like small children, explaining what we were about to do and then pausing to ask us if we had any questions. I wanted to know about the cotton balls, bad, but I decided to wait and see. In the very next moment, the woman of the house explained that we would begin by washing our hands, but since there were too many of us to do it properly, we would do it ceremonially, by dipping a cotton ball into the bowl of water and cleaning our hands with it right there in the dining room. It was not really about germs anyway, she explained. It was about coming before God with a clean heart.

Charmed by doing this new ritual for the first time, I stepped up to the bowl and dipped my cotton ball in the water. Then I moved out of the way so that others could follow. As the Christians all stood there quietly dabbing at our fingers with the Jews, I realized that this was one of the bones the Pharisees picked with Jesus, at least according to Matthew.

Then Pharisees and scribes came to Jesus from Jerusalem and said, "Why do your disciples break the tradition of the elders? For they do not wash their hands before they eat."

Matthew 15:1–2

I could not for the life of me connect the negative associations of the story with the positive thing that I was doing in that dining room. It was one of those revelations you have to be there for. It was an embodied epiphany. I was not *reading* about hand washing or discussing it in Bible study. I was *doing* it, among achingly generous people who experienced life in keeping the traditions of the elders. Because I was doing it with them, I found life in it too, which was the substance of my revelation.

From Matthew's time to my own, the hand washing itself was less the issue than who did it and how they encountered one another—with love or enmity, from the desire to include or divide? The issue was not the ritual but the relationships. Washing my hands did not make me a Jew, any more than it kept me from being a Christian. At the moment, it was simply a way of heading toward the edge of my own tradition in order to meet people who were reaching out to me from the edge of their own.

WHAT WE HAVE most in common is not religion but humanity. I learned this from my religion, which also teaches me that encountering another human being is as close to God as I may ever get—in the eye-to-eye thing, the person-to-person thing—which is where God's Beloved has promised to show up. Paradoxically, the point is not to see him. The point is to see the person standing right in front of me, who has no substitute, who can never be replaced, whose heart holds things for which there is no language, whose life is an unsolved mystery. The moment I turn that person into a character in my own story, the encounter is over. I have stopped being a human being and have become a fiction writer instead.

When I first came to Christian faith in college, people I barely knew made a habit of telling me they loved me. They were Christians too, and I guess it was their way of welcoming me to the family. I did not mind, exactly, but since they barely knew me I was not sure what they were talking about. Did they love the way my right foot turned out, so that I left tracks like a penguin on the beach? Did they love my willingness to make handprinted signs for Bible study? Did they love the way my upper lip disappeared when I laughed? I decided to find out, so the next time one of the Christians said she loved me, I asked her why.

She made a surprised face, like I should already know

"Because God loves you!" she said, throwing both hands in the air. "I love you because God loves everybody!"

This may sound small, but I decided that was not enough for me. I did not want to be loved in general. I wanted to be loved in particular, as I was convinced God loved. Plus, I am not sure it is possible to see the face of God in other people if you cannot see the faces they already have. What is it that makes that face different from every other face? If someone threw a blindfold over your own eyes right now, could you say what color those other eyes are? If you had to send someone into a crowded room to find this person, what detail would you use to make sure she was found?

The Desert Fathers did not see one another all that often, but when they did they knew the encounter would be holy. This did not mean that they always behaved particularly well; it just meant that they knew they were one another's best bets for becoming fully human. Once a brother went to one of the elders, saying:

There are two brothers, of whom one remains praying in his cell, fasting six days at a time and doing a great deal of penance. The other one takes care of the sick. Which one's work is more pleasing to God? The elder replied: If that brother who fasts six days at a time were to hang himself up by the nose, he could not equal the one who takes care of the sick.[11]

These brothers did all the things you would expect a bunch of monks to do: not just fasting and caring for the sick but also reading scripture, praying, bridling their tongues, and practicing charity. One of the more remarkable things they did was to cover one another's sins. When one of them was caught at something—say, having a girl in his room—one of the others would sit on the basket where she was hiding until the abbot inspector left the room. They behaved the same way with thieves who came to rob them of the little they had.

Once, when some robbers came into an elder's cell and told him they had come to take everything he had, he said, "My sons, take all you want." After they had stuffed everything they could find in their bags, they started off. But when the elder saw that they had left a little bundle hidden from view, he picked it up and chased after them.

"My sons, take this, you forgot it in the cell!" he shouted. The thieves were so amazed that they brought everything back, saying, "This one really is a man of God!"[12]

The nature of the encounter is apparently not important. What is important is that at least one person is willing to treat it as holy, capitalizing the "You" as well as the "I." If you have ever been on the receiving end of such an encounter, then you know how it can change you. By covering your sin—running after you with the one thing you forgot to steal—another human being can suck the malevolence right out of you, leaving you buck naked long enough to see another way of being held out in front of you and grab it. Sometimes you get to be the thief. Sometimes you get to be the holy person. Either way, the encounter changes you. It is what life is all about.

This practice is not designed to place you or those you love in danger, although it may help you discover how dangerous your own fear can be. The assignment is to get over your self. The assignment is to love the God you did not make up with all your heart, soul, strength, and mind, and the second is like unto it: to love the neighbor you also did not make up as if that person were your own strange and particular self. Do this, and the doing will teach you everything you need to know. Do this, and you will live.

7

The Practice of Living with Purpose

VOCATION

Do not be too moral. You may cheat yourself out of too much life. Aim above morality. Be not simply good; be good for something.

—*Henry David Thoreau*

I n my life so far, I have been a babysitter, an Avon lady, a cashier, a cheese-packer, a horseback riding instructor, a nursing unit clerk, a cocktail waitress, a secretary, a newspaper reporter, an editor, a fund-raiser, a special events coordinator, a teacher of creative writing, a hospital chaplain, a pastor, a preacher, and a college professor—and those are just the jobs that I have been paid for.

I still have not given up on becoming a chef, a jewelry maker, a travel writer, a zookeeper, a chambermaid, a bookstore manager, or—the most secret, thrilling vocational desire of all—a member of the French Canadian traveling circus Cirque du Soleil. I do not have my heart set on becoming an acrobat or anything. I would be happy selling tickets or managing props—anything that would let me play a part in the transformation that comes over ordinary, worn-out people when they go to the circus.

I have no defense for this largely frivolous list except that every job I have ever worked has brought me into contact with a crowd of people I might never have discovered any other way. Every job has required me to learn things that have opened up whole new dimensions of reality to me. Every job has revealed some ability I did not know I had, just as it has exposed some clumsiness I was pretty sure I had. While I was a cocktail waitress I once spilled a whole Singapore Sling down the back of an Australian woman's red fox coat. I also discovered how malignantly people can treat those who serve them, even when they do not get drinks dumped on them. There were nights I had to take a shower the moment I got home, not because of the grease and onion smells in my hair but because of the pure human meanness that covered me like truck exhaust. While I was a hospital chaplain I discovered that the sicker people were, the more they forgave my ineptness. After the doctors had left the room and there was nothing to do but die, a patient would often let me get by with sitting and watching television with her while we held hands.

Earlier in my life, I thought there was one particular thing I was supposed to do with my life. I thought that God had a purpose for me and my main job was to discover what it was. This thought heated up while I was in seminary, where I attended classes and drank beer with other students who knew exactly what they would do when they graduated. Upon request most of them could deliver articulate accounts of their calls to ministry. They took courses designed to prepare them to preach, teach, and deliver pastoral care. They had long lists of people willing to write recommendations for them when it came time for them to apply for their first jobs in parish ministry.

All I had was a love of what I was learning and the people I was learning it with. I loved the way the maple outside the dining hall turned fire-engine red in the fall. I loved learning biblical Hebrew. I loved a young man from Camden, New Jersey. I loved the professor who got so excited about what he was teaching that he fell straight backward in his chair. I loved going to daily chapel and sipping coffee afterward in a common room furnished with fragrant old leather sofas and oil portraits of the school's luminaries. I loved looking around the crowded common room wondering who would be the next luminaries, still so well disguised as students like me.

I did not have a single clue what I would do when I graduated. I did not even belong to a church. So I began asking God to tell me what I was supposed to do. What was my designated purpose on this earth? How could I discover the vocation that had my name on it? Since this was an important prayer, I searched for the right place to pray it. After a few lackluster attempts by the side of my bed and a few more in various cubbyholes around campus, I found a fire escape that hung precariously from the side of a deserted Victorian mansion next door to the Divinity School. That same night I crept over there after dark. Stepping over the "Danger: Keep Off" sign at the bottom, I climbed to the top, listening to the bolts creak as I tried to minimize the thundering of my feet on the narrow iron steps. I was so reluctant to take my hands off the rails that layers of old paint crackled under my palms like cornflakes. At the top I had to take a deep breath before I could let go of my handholds long enough to turn around. I did it as fast as a trapeze artist, gripping the rails again as soon as I sat down.

The fire escape turned out to be an excellent place to pray. Doing something that scared me cranked up my courage. Escaping up instead of down prepared me for other reversals. There was not a chance anyone could sneak up on me. The wind smelled like the moon. I went up there so many times in the weeks that followed that I no longer remember which night it was that God finally answered my prayer. I do not think it was right at the beginning, when I was still saying my prayers in words. I think it came later, when I had graduated to inchoate sounds. Up on that fire escape, I learned to pray the way a wolf howls. I learned to pray the way that Ella Fitzgerald sang scat.

Then one night when my whole heart was open to hearing from God what I was supposed to do with my life, God said, "Anything that pleases you."

"What?" I said, resorting to words again. "What kind of an answer is that?"

"Do anything that pleases you," the voice in my head said again, "and belong to me."

At one level, that answer was no help at all. The ball was back in my court again, where God had left me all kinds of room to lob it wherever I wanted. I could be a priest or a circus worker. God really did not care. At another level, I was so relieved that I sledded down the stairs that night. Whatever I decided to do for a living, it was not *what* I did but *how* I did it that mattered. God had suggested an overall purpose, but was not going to supply the particulars for me. If I wanted a life of meaning, then I was going to have to apply the purpose for myself.

Later, I would find the work of Martin Luther helpful in this regard. A monk who became convinced that no livelihood was dearer to the heart of God than any other, he left the monastery to proclaim the priesthood of all believers. Whatever our jobs in the world happen to be, Luther said, our mutual vocation is to love God and neighbor. "None of the things with which you deal daily are too trifling to tell you this incessantly," he wrote, "if you are but willing to hear it; and there is no lack of such preaching, for you have as many preachers as there are transactions, commodities, tools and other implements in your house and estate, and they shout this to your face: 'My dear, use me toward your neighbor as you would want him to act toward you with that which is his.'"[1]

With Luther's encouragement, I went on to use martini glasses on serving trays, saddles on spotted ponies, communion bread and wine, newspaper stories, bouquets of flowers delivered to nursing homes, suppers cooked for friends, checks from my checkbook, and green ink on student essays as purposeful means of engaging my vocation. Every one of these tools gave me ample opportunity to choose kindness over meanness. Every one of them offered me the chance to recognize the divine in human form, inviting me out of myself long enough to engage someone whose fears, wants, loves, and needs were at least as important as my own. Of course, they also gave me ample opportunity to act like a jerk, missing my purpose by a mile. Yet even this turned out to be helpful, since recognizing my jerkdom is how I remember that is not who I want to be.

IN MOST WAYS that count, I have been lucky in my work life. I have not lived on food stamps for more than a year. I have never had to declare bankruptcy. Even when I was so poor that I was stealing rolls of toilet paper from the place where I worked, I had an education to convince me that I was not as negligible as I sometimes felt. Whether I was typing someone else's letters at sixty words per minute or attending yet another meeting of the church finance committee, I kept the sense of purpose I discovered on that fire escape tucked in my pocket like the key to a safe deposit box.

I am no expert, but it seems to me that what many people are missing is a sense of purpose in their work. Some think it is money they are missing, or recognition, or congenial co-workers—and some of them are right. I know people who work so hard for so little that going to work simply reinforces their sense of not being worth much. Sometimes it takes two such jobs to feed a family of four, so that feeding the children means never seeing them. The work can also be deadly dull, the benefits nonexistent, and the boss a tyrant. If the work requires physical strength that cannot last forever, then the losses of age are multiplied by the loss of employment, with a disability check becoming one's best hope for the future.

Everyone deserves a decent job at a living wage with health care benefits for dependents. Yet even people who are well paid for their work can dread getting up in the morning. Several years ago, the physician Larry Dorsey observed that more heart attacks occur between 8:00 and 9:00 a.m. on Monday mornings than at any other time during the week.[2] To discover all the reasons for this phenomenon, you would have to interview every one of those heart attack patients individually, at least the ones who survived. You would also have to become a very good student of history, sociology, psychology, and economics, since work is a social reality as well as an individual one.

What interests me is the way that a person's work does or does not sustain that person's sense of purpose. My guess is that many people work at jobs that are too small for them. While the world deeply needs people who will punch cash registers, enter data, empty bedpans, and take household garbage to the dump, these purposes are too small for most human beings. People know when their gifts are being wasted, and this knowledge can eat away at the soul like a cancer. Call me a romantic, but I think most people want to be good for something. I think they want to do something that matters, to be part of something bigger than themselves, to give themselves to something that is meaningful instead of meaningless.

And yet meaningful work is hard to come by. Not everyone can teach school or cure illness. Plenty of us do not get the kind of work we want, and plenty more can find it difficult to stay focused on the meaning of what we are doing. A parent who spends his or her day changing diapers and scraping applesauce off a toddler's chin can have a hard time remembering that this unpaid work serves the purpose of forming a human being. A laborer for the department of transportation who spends hours pushing hot asphalt into potholes can have a hard time remembering that this work serves the purpose of keeping cars out of ditches on rainy nights.

In Buddhist teaching, right livelihood is one of the flagstones on the Noble Eightfold Path. Along with right speech, right intention, right action, and right effort, right livelihood is a key step in waking up to the true nature of reality, which includes the true nature of you. The inherited wisdom is that certain kinds of work are bad for you. Being a hired killer is not so good, for instance. Neither is selling drugs, arms, or sex. The basic principle is to do no harm. Beyond that, you are free to do quite a lot of things for a living, but they are not all going to come with their own evident purposes. Supplying that purpose is going to be up to you.

The Indian philosophy from which Buddhism sprang includes the notion of karma yoga—literally, the work path to God—one of

the many paths human beings have found that lead them deeper
into the divine. Gandhi walked this path when he sat down in
front of his spinning wheel to make thread for cloth that the British could not tax. Mother Teresa walked it when she knelt by the
bathtub in her hospice to wash someone fresh off the streets of
Calcutta. Someone who worked there for a while told me there
was a sign over the bathtub that said, "This is my body." Someone
else told me that Mother Teresa was not a pleasant person, which
helped keep volunteers focused on what they were doing instead
of on her.

Karma yogis approach their work as spiritual practice, whether
it is something as menial as spinning thread or something as
exalted as running a hospice. Since the point is to do useful work
unselfishly, menial tasks can work even better than exalted ones.
There is less possibility that your ego will get fat on packing groceries than on picking securities. There is less risk that you will
spend your time thinking about what kind of Lexus you are going
to buy with your next paycheck. "Desire for the fruits of work
must never be your motive in working," says the Bhagavad Gita.[3]
Your motive is to lose your self in your work, understanding that
it is possible to stack cans of beans on a grocery store shelf with
the consciousness of a spiritual master.

Work connects us to other people. This is obvious, for those
who work in service industries. A snarling customer calls for
the benevolence of a monk, at least if you do not want to seed an
epidemic of snarliness. Every human interaction offers you the
chance to make things better or to make things worse. To decide
to make things better can cost you bundles of self-interest. To
decide to make things worse generally feels a lot more powerful.
The only problem is that the power rolls away from you like a
rogue wave, as the person you slammed into finds someone else

to slam into, and so on, and so on. The good news is that you can set off the same sort of chain reaction with unwarranted kindness. Kindness is not a bad religion, no matter what name you use for God.

Work even connects solitary workers to other people. The writer sitting all alone in her room labors to choose exactly the right words for people she will never see. The night watchman stays awake so that others may sleep. The custodian who cleans empty classrooms at the elementary school creates a space into which tomorrow morning's loud children will come. If they do not notice her work, then that is because she maintains their eight-to-three world in ways they have come to count on. If the sun did not come up one day, they would notice.

No work is too small to play a part in the work of creation. At the Cirque du Soleil, the person who replaces the lightbulbs is vitally important to the high-wire artist, who must see where to put her foot. At the Ford plant, the person in charge of left front tire bolts is vitally important to the mother who drives her children to school each day. Since this connection is not always apparent, it calls for a little extra effort. Any worker with a good imagination should be able to come up with hundreds of people whom his or her work affects.

Yet it is always possible that one's true work in the world is not what one does for a living. Several years ago I watched a charming Swedish film called *My Life as a Dog*. One of the main characters worked in a glass factory, where the work was hot and somewhat tedious. I am sure he could think of a hundred people whom his work affected, but that was not where his heart was. His heart was with the boys on the village soccer team that he coached after work.

When his day's work was done, he ceased being a professional glassblower and became an amateur soccer coach. In his case, "amateur" did not mean that he was unskilled at coaching, although he was certainly unpaid. It meant that he loved what he was doing. Coaching was his *amore*, the thing that wedded his life to the lives of his players and the whole village for whom they played.

In a world where the paid work that people do does not always feed their hearts, it seems important to leave open the possibility that our vocations may turn out to be things we do for free. I know an attorney whose vocation is dressing up as Santa Claus every Christmas so the children in his small town can tell him their heart's desires. I know a teacher whose vocation is ironing sheets for hospice patients so their beds are as crisp as those in any four-star hotel.

While it is sometimes possible to turn your love into your work—especially if you can figure out how to live on less—that is not always the best idea. When the music you love to play becomes the music you have to play to pay the rent, your heart can suffer from alienation of affection. The poet Wallace Stevens worked for an insurance company by day. T. S. Eliot was a banker, and Philip Levine was a Detroit autoworker.

At least part of the beauty of unpaid work is that we choose to do it. In the midst of lives driven largely by compulsion, the choice to take on more work simply because we love doing it is an act of liberation. Many years ago now I met with the other clergy in my small town on a monthly basis. We whined a lot, as most clergy do, about how hard our jobs were. We also encouraged one another, pooling our wisdom about how to keep our sense of vocation alive.

I felt most deeply for my Baptist colleague, whose religious tradition compelled him to preach three different sermons every week without falling behind on all the other tasks of keeping a medium-sized church going. If he stayed home until noon to work on his sermons, people complained that he was not available. If he came to the office to work on his sermons, people knocked on his door all morning long. What saved this guy, as far as I could tell, was the clown outfit in his closet. On his day off, he put it on and went wherever he could make people laugh: children's hospitals, nursing homes, charity benefits. Without the makeup, he was a pretty serious fellow, so it made perfect sense that his exercise in freedom required a wild orange wig. One day he was telling us about his Saturday gig when the Presbyterian among us interrupted him.

"I just figured out what I'm missing," he said. "I mean, what the rest of you have that I don't. All of you do something else besides church." He was right. The Methodist was a volunteer fireman. The Catholic taught Italian at a community college. I wrote books. All of us were committed to parish ministry, which was our main vocation. What allowed us to keep answering the call to do it, however, was knowing that there was something else we could do too.

In my case, that knowledge helped me take risks I might not otherwise have taken. It also reminded me that while my chosen vocation gave me a really good job in the divine work of creation, it remained a subset of a larger vocation, which was the job of loving God and neighbor as myself. Over the years I have come to think of this as the vocation of becoming fully human.

Since some people consider being human a liability, and "fully" would only make things worse, I should perhaps explain what I mean. To become fully human means learning to turn my gratitude for being alive into some concrete common good. It means growing gentler toward human weakness. It means practicing forgiveness of my and everyone else's hourly failures to live up to divine standards. It means learning to forget myself on a regular basis in order to attend to the other selves in my vicinity. It means living so that "I'm only human" does not become an excuse for anything. It means receiving the human condition as blessing and not curse, in all its achingly frail and redemptive reality.

"The glory of God is a human being fully alive," wrote Irenaeus of Lyons some two thousand years ago. One of the reasons I remain a Christian-in-progress is the peculiar Christian insistence that God is revealed in humankind—not just in human form but also in human being. This insistence shows up most often in the Christian claim that God was made known in Jesus. In Jesus, Christians believe, everyone gets a good look at what it means to be both fully human and fully divine—not half and half, as if he walked around with a dotted line down his middle, but fully both, all the time. His full humanity was on full display as he taught, healed, fed, and freed people, just as it was when he honored the poor, defied the powerful, and turned the institutional tables along with his own cheek.

When I ask people to tell me how Jesus could be both fully human and fully divine, they often describe a kind of laminating process, in which his humanity was encased in divine plastic. The last thing to occur to most of us is that to be fully one is to be fully the other. What is it about "fullness" that we do not understand?

My advice is not to think about this too much, since thinking about it will not only make you crazy but will also take you out of the world where you can practice being fully human yourself. Jesus clearly thought this was the best plan. When people wanted him to tell them what God's realm was like, he told them stories about their own lives. When people wanted him to tell them God's truth about something, he asked them what they thought. With all kinds of opportunities to tell people what to think, he told them what to do instead. Wash feet. Give your stuff away. Share your food. Favor reprobates. Pray for those who are out to get you. Be the first to say, "I'm sorry." For those who took him as their model, being fully human became a full-time job. It became a vocation in itself, no matter what they happened to do for a living.

ONE COMMON PROBLEM for people who believe that God has one particular job in mind for them is that it is almost never the job they are presently doing. This means that those who are busiest trying to figure out God's purpose for their lives are often the least purposeful about the work they are already doing. They can look right through the people they work with, since those people are not players in the divine plan. They find ways to do their work without investing very much in it, since that work is not part of the divine plan. The mission to read God's mind becomes a strategy for keeping their minds off their present unhappiness, until they become like ghosts going through the motions of the people they once were but no longer wish to be.

Since I have felt that way myself, I have had to come up with ways to combat the ghostliness. The best cure is to find someone else's feet to wash, but failing that, washing almost anything will do. When old work has become meaningless and new purpose is hard to find, I recommend cleaning baseboards. In the first place, the warm water feels good on your hands. In the second place, you have to get down on your knees to do it. In the third place, the baseboards look terrific afterward, sometimes for as long as three months.

Washing a dog also works, although large dogs may require more despondence than you actually have to work off. Washing windows is also good. After drought sucked all the water out of my shallow well earlier this year, I began taking my dirty clothes to the Laundromat in town. The last time I did this was in 1978, which means that I took about a dozen quarters with me this time. After I had loaded up the biggest washer with bedsheets and added the detergent, I stared at the lit red number 18 by the coin slot. What could it mean? Was this the eighteenth washer in the Laundromat? Did the wash cycle require eighteen minutes? After a brief period of meditation I realized that I was meant to put eighteen quarters in the slot. *Eighteen quarters.* As it turned out, I got a whole afternoon of playing children, new neighbors, honest work, and sweet-smelling sheets for just a little over $4.50.

I no longer call such tasks housework. I call them *the domestic arts,* paying attention to all the ways they return me to my senses. When the refrigerator has nothing in it but green onions that have turned to slime and plastic containers full of historic leftovers, I know my art is languishing. When I cannot tell whether that is a sleeping cat or an engorged dust ball under my bed, I know that I have been spending too much time thinking. It is time to get down on my knees. After I have spent a whole morning ironing shirts, folding linens, rubbing orange-scented wax into wood, and cleaning dead bugs out of the light fixtures, I can hear the whole house purring for the rest of the afternoon. I can often hear myself singing as well, satisfied with such simple, domestic purpose.

This is my practice, not yours, so please feel free to continue calling such work utter drudgery. The point is to find something that feeds your sense of purpose, and to be willing to look low for that purpose as well as high. It may be chopping wood and it may be running a corporation. Whatever it is, perhaps you will hold open the possibility that doing it is one way to learn what it means to become more fully human, as you press beyond being good to being good for something, in a world with the perfect job for someone like you.

8

The Practice of Saying No

SABBATH

> God is not found in the soul by adding anything but by
> subtracting.
>
> —*Meister Eckhart*

A few years ago the bestseller list included a book on leadership called *Getting to Yes*. I think it was about moving from win-lose situations to win-win situations in which everyone involved had an easier time "getting to yes." The title appealed to me enough to buy the book, although I never read it. *Getting to Yes* was such a positive concept that even seeing it on my bookshelf cheered me up. *Yes* is one of those words capable of changing a life through the utterance of a single syllable.

"Yes, I want the job."

"Yes, I will marry you."

"Yes, it is my desire to be baptized."

At least part of the pleasure of saying yes is knowing that someone wants you—wants to be with you, wants you to do something that you do well, wants to do it with you. Saying yes is how you enter into relationship. It is how you walk through the door into a new room. It is how you create the future.

This may account for the seductiveness of the word, especially in a "can do" culture where the ability to do many things at high speed is not only an adaptive trait but also the mark of a successful human being. As much as most of us complain about having too much to do, we harbor some pride that we are in such demand. We admire people who are able to keep more balls in the air than we are, and when they drop one we instinctively avert our eyes. We feel their pain.

Meanwhile, technology opens up more opportunities than ever to say yes. Messages from high school friends you have not seen in thirty years show up in your inbox. They found you through Google and are eager to be back in touch. Political action groups want you to sign and circulate petitions for very good causes. People at work send you links to their blogs or invite you to join their circle of friends on MySpace. You cannot even sign on to Amazon.com without being shown the covers of some books that you may like based on your previous purchases.

For these reasons and more, it is difficult to find many advocates for the spiritual practice of saying no.

"No, I want to stay home tonight."

"No, I have enough work for now."

"No, I have all the possessions I can take care of."

Depending on your temperament, your cultural conditioning, and your circle of friends, negations like these can sound like death wishes. If there is nothing more you want to do or have, then why go on living? If you are going to say no to perfectly good opportunities for adding more to your life, then what is the point?

Maybe you have to be really, really tired before you can answer questions like those. Maybe you have to be deeply discouraged by never having time for all the things that need doing in this world—not just the important things, like spending time with the people you love, taking care of your health, and engaging in purposeful work (paid or unpaid) that gives you a chance to participate in the repairing of the world, but also the minor but non-negotiable things, like keeping up with the laundry, getting your oil changed, stocking the refrigerator with something other than fat-free yogurt and frozen pizza, remembering to send in your quarterly estimated tax payments, getting your teeth cleaned, taking the cat to the vet for her annual shots, and changing the sheets on your bed before they develop brown images of your sleeping body on them like those pictures of people caught in the lava of Vesuvius.

Since you are reading a book right now, it is possible that you are not this busy, or perhaps you have found time to read by pushing something else aside, so that you will be even busier tomorrow. Or maybe you are one of those people who has to hide the fact that you are not all that busy, since being busy is how our culture measures worth.

Someone just told me that in China, the polite answer to "How are you?" is "I am very busy, thank you." If you are very busy, then you must be fine. If you have more to do than you can do, and the list never gets done but only longer, then you must be very fine, because not only in China but also right here at home, successful people are busy people. Effective people are busy people. Religious people are busy people. For millions and millions of people, busy-ness is The Way of Life.

"How are you?"

"Busy like crazy, but what else is new? And you?"

Some busy people cannot even tell the difference between re-laxation and narcolepsy, because the minute they sit down in a quiet place alone, they nod off. If it happens while you are reading this book, please, do not think a thing about it. I know you do not sleep well. It does not make any sense, since you are exhausted, but the fact is that it is very hard for your body to go from fifth gear to off just because you say so—at least not without a little pharmaceutical help. It is hard to watch the eleven o'clock news with your heart wide open, letting in the misery of neighbors near and far, and then sleep soundly through the night. It is hard to dream rejuvenating dreams or sink into those deep-sea delta brain waves when you keep waking up at three o'clock—what is it about that hour?—to think about how many unanswered e-mails you have in your inbox, how much money you owe on your credit cards, or how odd your heartbeat sounds all of a sudden. Did it always give that little flip at the end, like a small, beached fish in the middle of your chest? Never mind. What kind of stove would you buy if you could have any kind of stove you wanted? An Aga? A Thermador? A Viking?

And there was evening and there was morning, the seventh day.

WHEN YOU LIVE in the desert, where the sand is so hot it can melt your flip-flops, your day begins when the sun goes down. Your day begins when the air cools, and the breeze stirs, and the little bit of water in the air turns into a fine mist that you can feel on your upper lip, as if the evening had been poured into a goblet for you to drink. When you live in the desert, working twice as hard as people who do not, to lead your flock to food, and water, and shade, your day begins when they all lie down, no longer

interested in following you but only in murmuring to one another until they can fall asleep and graze fields of clover in their
dreams. Your day begins when you too can lie down by the fire,
with nothing to do but trade tales with the others, or play a tune
on your reed flute while the children watch for shooting stars
over all your heads.

And there was evening and there was morning, the seventh day.

THE GREAT SWISS theologian Karl Barth once wrote, "A being
is free only when it can determine and limit its activity." By that
definition, I have a hard time counting many free beings among
my acquaintance. I know people who can do five things at once
who are incapable of doing nothing. I know people who are able
to decide what to do without being able to do less of it. Since I
have been one of those people, I know that saying no is a more
difficult spiritual practice than tithing, praying on a cold stone
floor, or visiting a prisoner on death row—because while all of
those worthy activities may involve saying no to something else
so that I can do them instead, they still amount to doing more
instead of less. Limiting my activity does not help me feel holy.
Doing more feels holy, which is why I stay so intrigued by the
fourth commandment.

Remember the Sabbath day and keep it holy. Six days you
shall labor and do all your work, but the seventh day is a
Sabbath of the LORD your God: you shall not do any work—
you, your son or your daughter, your male or female slave,
or your cattle, or the stranger who is within your settle-
ments. For in six days the LORD made heaven and earth and

A

sea, and all that is in them, and He rested on the seventh day; therefore the LORD blessed the Sabbath day and hallowed it.

Exodus 20:8–11, JPS Tanakh

The first time I really tried this was the Sunday after my last Sunday as a parish minister. After more than twenty years of being in church most Sunday mornings, I found myself suddenly faced with a whole day at home alone. I could not go to the church I had just resigned from. I did not want to go to church anywhere else. I thought about going to the grocery store, but I live in a small town where someone was bound to report that I had been seen buying cold cuts on my first Sunday morning away from church. So I stayed home instead, where I confronted grave questions about my professional identity, my human worth, and my status before God.

But that only lasted about an hour. After that, I went out on the front porch and said morning prayer with the birds. Then I read until lunchtime. Then I made an egg sandwich. Then I took a nap. By the time the sun went down, I realized that I had just observed my first true Sabbath in more than twenty years. In the years since then, I have made a practice of saying no for one whole day a week: to work, to commerce, to the Internet, to the car, to the voice in my head that is forever whispering, "More." One day each week, More God is the only thing on my list.

While reading up on a practice is no substitute for practicing it, I have also read enough to remember that the Sabbath has always been Saturday, not Sunday. By the lunar reckoning of the Bible, it starts on Friday evening and it ends on Saturday evening. Look the word up in the book of Exodus and you discover that Jews were observing Sabbath *before* Moses brought the stone tablets of God's holy law down from Mount Sinai. The first holy thing in all creation, Abraham Heschel says, was not a people or a place but a day. God made everything in creation and called it good, but when God rested on the seventh day, God called it holy. That makes the seventh day a "palace in time," Heschel says, into which human beings are invited every single week of our lives.[1]

Why are we so reluctant to go?

I can think of several reasons, beginning with how some of us were raised. If you are of a certain age and were raised in the South, then for all practical purposes the commandment might as well have read, "Remember the Sabbath day, and keep it boring." The Sabbath was the day you could not wear blue jeans, could not play ball, could not ride bikes, could not go to the movies, could not do anything but go to church in the morning and *again* at night, with a wasteland in between during which old people with little hair left on their heads but a great deal growing out of their ears sat around in rocking chairs talking about incredibly dull things and you could not creep away for more than twelve minutes without your mother yelling, "What are you *doing* in there? Come back out here and visit with your Uncle Lynch and Aunt Alma, who came all the way from East Point to see you."

Sabbath was the day you *could not,* because the Bible said so. If I knew then what I know now, I would have argued more, since the Bible does not say one thing about resting on *Sunday.* Biblically speaking, the Sabbath has always been Saturday, and the Lord's Day has always been Sunday, the day when Christian tradition holds that Jesus was raised from the dead. There is evidence that for a very little while, early Christians tried to observe both the Sabbath and the Lord's Day. They rested on Saturday and gathered to remember the resurrection on Sunday. Then the

church and the synagogue got a nasty divorce and part of the
separation agreement was the division of holy days.

This explains how most Christians grow up thinking of
Sunday as the Sabbath, but it does not make them any better at
saying no on that day or any other. Until about fifty years ago,
Southern culture made Sabbath practice easier by not offering
any alternatives. Movie theaters and municipal swimming pools
were closed on Sundays. If you needed a cup of flour for the
baking-soda biscuits you were making for Sunday dinner, then
you were flat out of luck unless your neighbor had one to spare.
When you got through eating lunch you threw a big white sheet
over the dining room table to keep the flies off until supper, because no restaurants were open on Sundays. You did not even
hear the whistle of freight trains in Georgia on Sundays, because
it was illegal to haul goods on the Sabbath.

When Alexis de Tocqueville visited the United States in 1840,
he wrote of the Christian Sabbath, "Not only have all ceased to
work, but they appear to have ceased to exist."[2]

If he had come back in the 1960s, he would not have recognized
the place. More than 90 percent of homes had television sets by
then, and almost 40 percent of them were tuned to Sunday foot-
ball. The gross domestic product had become the foremost indica-
tor of the nation's health and well-being. Entertainments and shops
of every kind were open on Sundays, as the culture reneged on its
"no compete" clause with the church. Merchants were no longer
willing to stay closed to help churches stay open. People of faith
were free to keep the Sabbath if they wanted to, but not because
there was nothing else to do. They would have to make their own
choices from now on. They would have to find the strength to say
no for their own reasons, from their own spiritual resources, to
things that would from now on be easily within their reach.

While this seismic change spelled loss for some people, it spelled liberation for others. In Karl Barth's language, these Sunday captives were tired of other people determining how they would spend their Sabbaths. They welcomed the freedom to determine their own activities, and they set about making full use of their newfound sovereignty to work, shop, play, eat out, and haul freight to their hearts' content.

I guess I do not have to tell you how well that went. Once merchants began opening on Sundays, they needed people to work on Sundays as well. While higher-wage earners could say, "Thanks, I think I'll play golf instead," lower-wage earners had to choose between keeping the Sabbath and keeping their jobs. Either way, if people were going to work on Sundays, then it did not make much sense to say the kids could not play competitive sports on Sundays. And if the kids were going to play sports on Sundays, then someone was going to have to drive them, which was going to make pulling a meal together harder to do, but no harder than pulling the family together to sit down and eat together even once a week.

What happened to the American weekend also happened to the week. By the 1990s, the average worker was putting in 164 extra hours of paid labor each year—the equivalent of an extra month of work. Around this same time, the two-income household was becoming the middle-class norm, which meant that the new pressure at work was matched by new pressure at home. The incline in work time was matched by a steep decline in the unpaid activities on which most societies depend: the care of the very old and the very young, civic duties, volunteer work, church work, and support of the arts. While those who still bowled, bowled alone, Hallmark developed a new line of cards for absent parents. "Sorry I can't be here to tuck you in," one said. "Sorry I can't say good morning," read another.

According to Craig Harline, who has written a cultural history called *Sunday: A History of the First Day from Babylonia to the Super Bowl,* "Sundays changed when the world changed."[3] And according to his reviewer in the *Wall Street Journal,* "Stopping farming in the Middle Ages was easy. But to close restaurants, shut up amusement parks or clear the airwaves when Americans with money were trying to spend it that day was impossible."[4]

There is no talking about the loss of the Sabbath, then, without also talking about the rise of consumerism. There is no talking about Sabbath rest without also talking about Sabbath resistance. Since I am technically a Lord's Day Christian, I have no authority to speak of the Jewish Sabbath, but I freely indulge in what I call "holy envy." When I find something in another religious tradition that sets my heart on fire, I do not admonish myself for wishing it were mine. One thing I wish were mine is a proper Friday evening Shabbat service, beginning with the lighting of two candles when three stars can be counted in the darkening sky. According to those who know, there is one candle for each of the Sabbath commandments in Torah, both of which call God's people to be more like God.

The first commandment is based on the creation account in Genesis. You can tell that by the way it ends: "For in six days the Lord made heaven and earth and sea, and all that is in them, and He rested on the seventh day; therefore the Lord blessed the Sabbath day and hallowed it." God worked hard for six days and then God rested, performing the consummate act of divine freedom by doing nothing at all. Furthermore, the rest was so delicious that God did not call it good, or even very good. Instead, God blessed the seventh day and called it holy, making Sabbath the first sacred thing in all creation. Resting every seventh day, God's people remember their divine creation.

That is what the first Sabbath candle announces: *made in God's image, you too shall rest.*

The second candle stands for the second formulation of the Sabbath commandment in Deuteronomy 5. There the basis of the command shifts from the creation of the world to the exodus from Egypt, ending this way: "Remember that you were a slave in the land of Egypt and the LORD your God freed you from there with a mighty hand and an outstretched arm; therefore the LORD your God has commanded you to observe the Sabbath day." God's people cried out to God and God heard them, sending Moses to free them from bondage in a land that was not home. Resting every seventh day, God's people remember their divine liberation. That is what the second Sabbath candle announces: *made in God's image, you too are free.*

When observant Jews light two candles on Shabbat, they light one for each of these "therefores"—a rest candle and a freedom candle—which have more to do with each other than may be apparent at first. By interrupting our economically sanctioned social order every week, Sabbath practice suspends our subtle and not so subtle ways of dominating one another on a regular basis. Because our work is so often how we both rank and rule over one another, resting from it gives us a rest from our own pecking orders as well. When the Wal-Mart cashier and the bank president are both lying on picnic blankets at the park, it is hard to tell them apart. When two sets of grandparents are at the lake with their grandchildren feeding ducks, it is hard to tell the rich ones from the poor ones.

If Bible lovers paid as much attention to Leviticus 25 as to Leviticus 18, then we might discover that God is at least as interested in economics as in sex. According to that astounding chapter of Torah, Sabbath is not only about getting a little rest but also about freeing slaves, forgiving debts, restoring property, and giving the land every seventh year off.

> Six years you may sow your field and six years you may prune your vineyard and gather in the yield. But in the seventh year the land shall have a sabbath of complete rest, a sabbath of the LORD: you shall not sow your field or prune your vineyard. You shall not reap the aftergrowth of your harvest or gather the grapes of your untrimmed vines; it shall be a year of complete rest for the land. But you may eat whatever the land during its sabbath will produce—you, your male and female slaves, the hired and bound laborers who live with you, and your cattle and the beasts in your land may eat all its yield.
>
> *Leviticus 25:3–7, JPS Tanakh*

Sabbath is not only God's gift to those who have voices to say how tired they are; Sabbath is also God's gift to the tired fields, the tired vines, the tired vineyard, the tired land. Leviticus 25 shows divine concern for *grapes,* for God's sake. It promises both the tame and wild animals in the land enough to eat, along with the hired hands who presumably have time to take up wood-working and water aerobics during the year that the tractors stay parked in the barn.

SABBATH IS THE GREAT EQUALIZER, the great reminder that we do not live on this earth but in it, and that everything we do under the warming tent of this planet's atmosphere affects all who are woven into this web with us. Just because the land and the livestock cannot hire lawyers does not mean they have not been violated. Their biblical rights are written down right there in the Bible, but other gods go on getting in the way.

Where there is money to be made, there is no rest for the land, nor for those who live on it. In the rural county where I live, developers bulldoze the laurels by the river where the raccoons taught their babies how to fish. An entire pine forest comes down to produce the paper for one mail-order catalog. People who have already run out of closet space work overtime to pay the interest on their average $9,000 credit card debts, while economic predators send teenagers applications for their own preapproved cards in the mail. No resistance to such ravenousness will come from those who are heavily invested in its revenue. The resistance will have to come from elsewhere, from those who live by a different rhythm because they worship a different God.

In the eyes of the world, there is no payoff for sitting on the porch. A field full of weeds will not earn anyone's respect. If you want to succeed in this life (whatever your "field" of endeavor), you must spray, you must plow, you must fertilize, you must plant. You must never turn your back. Each year's harvest must be bigger than the last. That is what the earth and her people are for, right? *Wrong god.*

In the eyes of the true God, the porch is imperative—not every now and then but on a regular basis. When the fields are at rest—when shy deer step from the woods to graze the purple clover grown up between last year's tomato plants, and Carolina chickadees hang upside down to pry seeds from the sunflowers that have taken over the vineyard—when the people who belong to this land walk through it with straw hats in their hands instead of hoes to discover that wild blackberries water their mouths as surely as the imported grapes they worked so hard to protect from last year's frost—this is not called "letting things go"; this is called "practicing Sabbath." You have to wonder what makes human beings so resistant to it.

"Look at the birds of the air," Jesus once said, "they neither sow nor reap nor gather into barns, and yet your heavenly Father feeds them. Are you not of more value than they? And can any of you by worrying add a single hour to your span of life? And why do you worry about clothing? Consider the lilies of the field, how they grow; they neither toil not spin, yet I tell you, even Solomon in all his glory was not clothed like one of these."[5]

Sabbath is the true God's gift to those who wish to rest and to be free—and who are willing to guard those same gifts for every living thing in their vicinity as well. Remember the commandment? It is not just for you. It is for your children, your employees, your volunteer helpers, your hunting dogs, your plow horses, your fields, and your migrant workers. It does not matter in the least whether they believe in your God. You do, so they get the day off. Anyone who engages this practice discovers saving habits of work and rest that promise life not only for each of us individually but also for our families, our communities, our far-flung neighbors, our systems of justice, our human economies, and our planet.

According to the rabbis, those who observe Sabbath observe all the other commandments. Practicing it over and over again they become accomplished at saying no, which is how they gradually become able to resist the culture's killing rhythms of drivenness and depletion, compulsion and collapse. Worshiping a different kind of God, they are shaped in that God's image, stopping every seven days to celebrate their divine creation and liberation. And yet those who practice Sabbath, a little or a lot, know that there is another kind of resistance at work.

One of my favorite prayers in *Gates of Prayer,* the New Union Prayer Book, is called "Welcoming Sabbath" and it goes like this:

Our noisy day has now descended with the sun beyond our
   sight.

In the silence of our praying place we close the door upon the
   hectic joys and fears, the accomplishments and anguish of
   the week we have left behind.

What was but moments ago the substance of our life has
   become memory; what we did must now be woven into
   what we are.

On this day we shall not do, but be.

We are to walk the path of our humanity, no longer ride un-
   seeing through a world we do not touch and only vaguely
   sense.

No longer can we tear the world apart to make our fire.

On this day heat and warmth and light must come from deep
   within ourselves.[6]

If you can hear the welcome in that prayer, then perhaps you
can hear the dis-ease in it as well. How is your own deep fire
doing, by the way? Are you pretty confident that you have enough
heat and warmth and light within yourself to get you through the
night? Once you have turned off the computer and hung up the
car keys, once you have decided to take one whole day off from
earning your own salvation, are you ready to wrestle with the
brawny angels who show up?

A couple of years ago, the *New York Times* magazine ran an
article called "Bring Back the Sabbath" by Judith Shulevitz.[7] She
opened her piece by citing the work of Sandor Ferenczi, a disci-
ple of Freud's who worked in Budapest in the early 1900s. What

Ferenczi noticed was how many people came to see him complaining about the sudden onset of headaches, stomachaches, and attacks of depression they experienced every Sunday—or, in the case of his Jewish clients, every Saturday. After he had ruled out purely physical causes, including the rich Hungarian food served on these days, Ferenczi concluded that his patients were suffering from the Sabbath.

He called it "Sunday neurosis," attributing it to the loss of control people experienced on the Sabbath. When the shops shut down, so did "the machinery of self-censorship," he said. As the routines of the workweek gave way to family get-togethers, worship, and rest, Sunday neurotics feared that their wilder impulses might get away from them. With the "eternal inner murmur of self-reproach" temporarily silenced within them, they worried that they might run amok. So they produced bellyaches and the blues to protect them from the full freedom of the Sabbath.

Anyone who practices Sabbath for even an afternoon usually suffers a little spell of Sabbath sickness. Try it and you too may be amazed by how quickly your welcome rest begins to feel like something closer to a bad cold. Okay, that was nice. Okay, you are ready to get back to work now. Yes, you know you said you wanted this, but now you have had just the right amount of rest—maybe even a touch too much—so that you are beginning to feel sluggish. What if your energy level drops and never comes back up again? What if you get used to this and want never to go back to work? Plus, how will you ever catch up after taking a whole day off? Just thinking about it makes you tired.

Is weeding the garden really work if you enjoy it? Is looking through a Garnet Hill catalog really shopping? This, I think, is how the rabbis were finally forced to spell out all the kinds of work that are forbidden on the Sabbath—because people kept trying to find ways to get to yes instead of no. If I am a doctor and someone calls for help, am I allowed to help? If my dog gets sick, can I take her to the vet? Is striking a match really making a fire?

Yes, it is. If you decide to live on the fire God has made inside of you instead, then it will not be long before some other things flare up as well. Most of us move fast enough during the week to outrun them, but if you slow down for a day, then all kinds of alarming things can happen. You can start crying without having the slightest idea why. You can start remembering what you loved about people who died before you were ten, along with things you did when you were eighteen that still send involuntary shivers up your back. You can make a list of the times you almost died in your life, along with the reasons you are most glad to be alive.

Released from bondage to the clock, you eat when you are hungry instead of when you have to. Nine times out of ten you discover that you are far less hungry than you thought you were, or at least less for groceries than for the bread no one can buy. As you slow down, your heart does too. The girdle of your dia-phragm loosens, causing great sighs too deep for words to pour from your body. In their wake, you discover more room around your heart, a greater capacity for fresh air. Sabbath sickness turns out to be a lot like other sicknesses, which until now have been the only way you could grant yourself more than one day off from work. If you flee from the pain and failure, then you run into them everywhere you go. If you can find some way to open to them instead, then they may bring their hands from behind their backs and lay flowers on your bed.

Most people I know want to talk about why it is impossible for them to practice Sabbath, which is an interesting spiritual exercise in itself. If you want to try it, then make two lists on one piece of paper. On one side of the paper, list all of the things you *know* give you life that you never take time to do. Then, on the other side, make a list of all the reasons why you think it is impossible for you to do those things. That is all there is to it. Just make the two lists, and keep the piece of paper where you can see it. Also promise not to shush your heart when it howls for the list it wants.

If a whole day of life-giving freedom is too much for you to imagine, then start however you can. Decide that you will get up an hour before everyone else in the house and dedicate that time to doing nothing but being in the divine presence. Decide that you will turn off the television an hour before you go to bed and spend that time outside looking at the sky. You could resolve not to add anything more to your calendar without subtracting something from it. You could practice praising yourself for saying no as lavishly as you do when you say yes.

If you do any of these things, you will likely discover that they are very difficult to sustain all by yourself. It is hard to be a lone revolutionary, yet that is what you become when you start saying no. You rise up against your history, your ego, your culture and its ravenous economy. You may also have to rise up against your church or synagogue, if you belong to one, since such institutions can demand as much of you as any pharaoh. My advice is to find yourself a partner revolutionary. Find a whole community of revolutionaries if you can. They will help you hang on to your vision, the one that helps you remember who you were created to be. They may even supply you with some missing details, along with the support to realize them.

In the meantime, I think it is good to have a Sabbath vision even if it seems impossible to you right now. Here is mine, which you are free to borrow while you are envisioning your own.

At least one day in every seven, pull off the road and park the car in the garage. Close the door to the toolshed and turn off the computer. Stay home not because you are sick but because you are well. Talk someone you love into being well with you. Take a nap, a walk, an hour for lunch. Test the premise that you are worth more than what you can produce—that even if you spent one whole day being good for nothing you would still be precious in God's sight—and when you get anxious because you are convinced that this is not so, remember that your own conviction is not required. This is a *commandment*. Your worth has already been established, even when you are not working. The purpose of the commandment is to woo you to the same truth.

It is hard to understand why so many people put "Thou shalt not do any work" in a different category from "Thou shalt not kill" or "Thou shalt have no other gods before me," especially since those teachings are all on the same list. The ancient wisdom of the Sabbath commandment—and of the Christian gospel as well—is that there is no saying yes to God without saying no to God's rivals. No, I will not earn my way today. No, I will not make anyone else work either. No, I will not worry about my life, what I will eat or what I will drink, or about my body, what I will wear. Is not life more than food, and the body more than clothing? And there was evening and there was morning, the seventh day.

WHEN YOU LIVE IN GOD, your day begins when you open your eyes, though you have done nothing yourself to open them, and you take your first breath, though there is no reason why this life-giving breeze should be given to you and not to some other. In the dark or in the light, with a stone slab under your back or a feather topper, your day begins when you let God hold you because you do not have the slightest idea how to hold yourself— when you let God raise you up, when you consent to rest to show you get the point, since that is the last thing you would do if you were running the show yourself. When you live in God, your day begins when you lose yourself long enough for God to find you, and when God finds you, to lose yourself again in praise.

9

The Practice of
Carrying Water

PHYSICAL LABOR

He who is aching in every limb, worn out by the effort of a day of work, that is to say a day when he has been subject to matter, bears the reality of the universe in his flesh like a thorn. The difficulty for him is to look and to love. If he succeeds, he loves the Real.

—*Simone Weil*

When I lived in the city, a power outage meant eating sandwiches by candlelight for supper and going to bed early under a few extra quilts. When I moved to the country, a power outage meant hard labor for however many days it took the repair trucks to reach the end of my dirt road.

The first time this happened, the storm began with a beautiful, heavy snow. My husband, Ed, and I wasted no time getting out in it, charmed by the transformation of our dappled land into such smooth whiteness. Our Jack Russell terrier ran along the ground with her mouth open, making her own snow cones, while the horses pawed holes in the white stuff to make sure there was still grass underneath. The llamas frolicked like four-year-olds, reminded—at least genetically—of their ancestral life in the Andes. They were built for the cold. It was heat they could not stand.

After our walk Ed and I built a fire, hoping for enough snow to keep us home the next day. We had books to read, love to make, rest to catch up on. Snow was as good as Sabbath, maybe better, if it lasted longer than a day. While we were eating dinner, all of the lights in the house dimmed as if a movie were about to begin. Then they went out, accompanied by the dying beep of every appliance in the house.

Overnight, the snow turned to freezing rain. By morning, the yard looked as if the Ice Queen had crashed her sled right through the trees. Massive limbs littered the ground. The trees that had not snapped in two were bent over to the ground. The loblolly pines were the worst. Since they keep their needles through the winter, they have plenty of places for ice to collect. Pines do not belong in the mountains. They should all move to Florida, where they can grow old in peace.

The snowy footprints we had left on the mudroom steps were gone, replaced by a thick inch of ice on each tread. Simply to walk down them required a rock climber's nerve. At the bottom, we steadied each other until we gained enough confidence to walk. Then we set off down the two-mile stretch of dirt road that connected us to the highway. We walked past neighbors' cars in ditches and the splintered trunks of broken trees. We ducked under the frozen branches of those that had fallen across the road, breaking their coated needles with our bodies. Toothpicks of ice fell down the necks of our down jackets. The air was redo-lent with pine sap.

We counted eight substantial trees across the road before we came to the place where the tangle of electrical wires hung from a utility pole, their snapped ends coiled in the snowy roadbed like snakes.

Since we rely on an electric pump to draw water from our well, we knew this meant the end of running water as well as heat, light, and refrigeration. Turning around, we walked back in silence as each of us did the math: nine miles of downed power lines between us and the county generator divided by twenty-four hours plus however long it took to chainsaw eight fallen trees. Whatever else we had planned to do that week had just been canceled. Whatever else we did for a living, we had just become common laborers. On the way home we divided the work. Ed would keep the fire in the living room going, set up the kerosene heater in the garage for the outdoor dogs, and haul water from the frost-free pump down at the barn. I would nail quilts over the doors and windows of the living room, collect enough candles and flashlights to navigate after dark, and keep the animals, in-cluding the two of us, fed and watered.

I still had a small stockpile of dusty Y2K supplies that turned out to be useful after all. I loaded AA batteries into headlamps and tried out my hand-cranked, solar-powered radio, which predicted high winds and temperatures in the teens for the next several days. For dinner I opened a can of garbanzo beans, then tried to read by the light of a gas lamp. Growing dizzy, I checked the small print on the fuel can, which read: "Danger: for outdoor use only. Fumes are known by the state of California to cause cancer." Giving up for the night, I lowered myself into my sleep-ing bag on the living room couch. My terrier—who had never seen a sleeping bag in her life—made a sudden leap for the opening, burrowed her way down to the bottom, and curled up beside my socked feet with a sigh.

By morning the houseplants near windows were frozen. The inside of the refrigerator was warmer than the house, and the food inside of it was starting to smell funky. After eating a bowl of cereal with gloves on, I began boiling water, both to thaw the horses' drinking water and to warm food for the outside dogs. The water I set out at 9:00 a.m. was frozen by noon. When I found the horses licking ice, I promised to break the water in their trough with a hammer at least twice a day. Since the chicken waterers were smaller, they required smashing more often. The dogs were fine in the garage. The cats were as unaffected by the ice storm as they were by anything else. What was there to eat for lunch?

Rehearsing the various cycles of these physical needs in my mind, I felt my body expand. Was this how it felt to be a mother? It was no longer enough for me to be aware of my own bodily distress. Other lives depended on my awareness of their distress as well. By the end of the first day, I could respond without thinking. I knew when the dogs needed warm water as well as I knew when the horses needed their blankets. Necessity bound us together. It was our common language, one that did not require words.

By day two I dreaded the setting of the sun, when everything got colder and harder to do. I wore my headlamp everywhere I went, but it provided no more than a small circle of light. If I did not look directly at an object, it receded into shadow. I trod on things underfoot with no idea what they were. I learned to recognize the sweaters in my closet by feel instead of sight. Everywhere I turned, the darkness exposed my helplessness. I could not watch a movie, could not work on my computer, could not do laundry, could not take a bath, could not even walk across a room without fear of bashing my shin. I had lost power. I was without power. I had no power.

On day three, I decided that a power outage would make a great spiritual practice. Never mind giving up meat or booze for Lent. For a taste of real self-denial, just turn off the power for a while and see if phrases such as "the power of God" and "the light of Christ" sound any different to you. Better yet, ask someone to flip the switch *for* you and then cut the wire for good measure, thereby depriving you of the power to flip it back on again.

Live as most people in the world live, preoccupied with survival. Wear the same clothes for a week because it is too cold to think about taking them off. Sleep as close to the fire as you can, welcoming the heat of another human body. Learn to shake your head at goals such as higher education, aerobic fitness, computer proficiency, and self-fulfillment. Long for the light you cannot procure for yourself, and feel your heart swell with gratitude—every single morning—when the sun comes up. Value warmth. Prize shelter. Praise the miracle of flowing water.

On the afternoon of day four, just as I had finished deodorizing the empty refrigerator, there was a loud click, followed by the sound of a dozen engines coming on. I stood up. The yellow sponge fell from my hand. "*We have power!*" I shouted, with tears springing from my eyes. There should be a service in the prayer book for occasions such as these.

O God of the burning bush, we praise you for the return of
    heat and light.
O God of streams in the wilderness, we thank you for the gift
    of flowing water.

I do not wish for ice storms, either for myself or for anyone else. Yet I stay grateful for what this particular ice storm required of me. Having no power, I discovered how much I could actually do. I was made to exceed my self-interest for a while, expanding my circle of concern to include every living thing in my vicinity. I was deprived of my usual defenses against cold, darkness, and hardship, giving me a better sense of how most people live. I was forced to engage the brute requirements of staying alive on frozen earth, leading me to fresh appreciation of a body that works.

Long after the thaw, I stay tuned to the grace of physical labor. Bending and rising to hang laundry on the line, kneeling to scrub the yellow pollen off the back porch, hauling bales of fragrant hay up the steps to the loft, raking the chicken pens and gathering the eggs: this work gives me life. I choose to labor, of course, which sets me apart from those who have no such choice. With them, I live in a culture that regards physical labor as the lowest kind of work.

Gardening seems to be acceptable, along with washing the car and working out at the gym, but beyond that the general idea is to make enough money that you can pay other people to change your sheets, clean your toilets, mow your lawn, and raise your food. Typically, the people who do these things for a living are at the bottom of the economic ladder. If American culture admitted to caste, then these laborers would be the *shudras.*

Even those who do their own maintenance tend to collect labor-saving devices: dust-suckers, leaf-blowers, dish-washers, weed-eaters. Enormous people ride across their lawns on mowers equipped with cold beer holders. People with noise-reducing headphones on their heads strafe their driveways with hideously loud machines, blowing leaves into the street that the first passing car will blow back into their yards again. Do children ever leap into piles of raked leaves anymore? Are teenagers still made to mow lawns when they miss their curfews? It is difficult to imagine this last bit working with a riding mower, but perhaps the very idea of physical labor is enough to ruin a teenager's day.

I have an eleven-year-old friend who grew up on computers. At three, he knew how to work the remote key to my car. By the time he was six, he was so quick on the trigger of his video games that no adult could best him. He was so quick, in fact, that it became difficult for him to focus on anything for more than a few seconds before he was off to something else. When his parents brought him to my house, he came equipped with his DVD player, his Game Boy, and various electrical toys used for hand-to-hand combat. I played one with him that involved pressing buttons on a remote control so that my plastic boxer flailed his arms and feet with the object of knocking his plastic boxer down. By the time I figured out how the buttons worked, my plastic boxer was lying face up on the ground with his fists punching air. My young friend crowed with victory. He had won again.

I do not remember how we ended up digging potatoes. I think I refused to play anything else that required batteries and he sullenly followed me to the barn, where I showed him how to collect the eggs that the hens had laid. After that we gave the chickens some corn and the horses some hay. He brightened up when we boarded the Gator to ride to the garden. He wanted to drive. I pointed to the warning on the dashboard, which pretty much guaranteed we would die if anyone under sixteen were allowed to drive the Gator. Then I hit the gas along with every bump I could find, so that he could focus his attention on trying to keep his seat instead of wanting to drive.

You know it is time to dig the potatoes when their leaves start to turn brown. Ed taught me this the first time I dug potatoes with him, which I still remember with perfect clarity. Like my young friend, I was reluctant to be in the garden. I did not want to get dirt under my fingernails. I did not want to sweat. I wanted to be indoors doing something that involved books or at least newsprint. But Ed was so excited by the prospect that I might be excited by digging potatoes that I relented just to shut him up, complaining bitterly all the way to the garden.

He picked up a shovel and loosened the dirt at the base of a shriveled-looking plant.

"Dig there," he said. I gave him a withering look.

"Go on," he said. "Just see what you can find."

I stuck my hands in the dirt and started feeling around. The dirt was damp and cool. It smelled fresh and mysterious. I broke clods apart with my fingers, waiting for something that felt like a potato. Since I could not see what I was doing under the earth, I looked at the trees instead. I looked at the leaning pines, the heavy oaks, the straight poplars, the gnarled dogwoods. I looked at the blue sky through their branches, all the while working the dirt beneath my hands.

My first potato was the size of a marble—a big one, a shooter—still attached to its mother by a root no thicker than a broom straw.

"It's just a baby," I said to Ed. "Should I leave it alone?"

"The plant is finished," he said. "You can have everything you find." So I popped the root and put the potato in my bucket, plunging my hands back into the earth. There was a whole nest of small potatoes right behind my first find. I dug them out and brushed them off, every one of them a different shape. When I dropped them in the bucket they thumped the bottom like a small cloud of hailstones.

Reaching back into the dirt, I felt something curved poking out from the wall of the hole that Ed had dug. Little by little I cleared away the earth around it, drawing out handfuls of dirt with earthworms in them. My fingernails were wrecked. I went back in. Gradually the curve became half a sphere. My shoulders were cramping. I kept digging until I had freed a potato as big as my hand. Brushing the dirt off of its yellow skin, I understood why the potato was called a Yukon Gold. I had never seen anything so elementally good-looking that passed for food.

After that, I was unstoppable. Digging potatoes was like playing the slots in Vegas. I never knew what I would get. Sometimes it was change and sometimes I hit big. The gamble was half the fun. The exertion was the other half—the difficult, physical labor of drawing food from the ground. That night, when Ed and I sat down to a pan of roasted potatoes with Jerusalem artichokes and whole garlic, I hurt so badly that I could hardly lift my fork to my mouth. When I did, I ate the whole day: the fragrant dirt, the blue sky, the dying potato plant, its golden offspring. I had never tasted anything so nourishing in all my life.

My young friend preferred French fries to roasted potatoes, but he was as taken as I was with locating their source. Like many his age, he had never made the connection between what he ate and where it came from. If you had told him that grapefruits grow on trees, he would not have believed you. Once he learned the potato routine, however, he dug in the dirt with perfect focus, visibly pleased with his ability to produce real food. I am not sure that he had ever felt genuinely useful before. The next time he came to see me, he still brought all his electrical stuff but he left it in the car.

"Can we dig potatoes?" he asked.

THERE IS NO substitute for earthiness. From dust we came and to dust we shall return. The good news is that most of us get some good years in between, during which we may sink our hands in the dirt. This is as good a way as any to recover our connection to the ground of all being. Digging down is as good a way to God as rising up, if only because you can feel it in your shoulders.

I have taken biblical Hebrew twice in my life, once in college and once in graduate school. Both times, I quit when I got to verbs. Nouns exhausted my memory bank, as well as my capacity for awe. One of the first nouns I learned was "earthling." Having grown up on the King James Version of the Bible, I was greatly affected by the knowledge that God did not make "man" in the second chapter of Genesis. God made *adam*—an earthling—from the *adamah*—the earth. God made a mud-baby, a dirt-person, a dust-creature. Then God breathed into its nostrils, giving it divine CPR, and behold! A living being arose from the ground.

The next thing God did was to plant a garden in that same ground. Then God made trees grow out of the ground that were pleasant to look at and good for food. Finally, God put the earthling on that patch of earth to till it and keep it. This was before all the trouble with the snake. This was even before the earthling had a partner. When God determined that it was not good for the earthling to be alone, God fashioned a companion from the earthling's bone—bone made from the minerals of the earth—and presented the companion to the earthling. The companion did not require divine CPR, apparently. The companion was live from the start.

It is only at this point in the story that the *ish*—the man—is distinguished from the *ishah*—the woman. One word will not suffice for two creatures of such elegant distinction. Still, both of these earthlings come from the same source. Call it ground or call it God. The life they share comes from the same place. Later, after the incident with the snake, God evicts these two from the garden. Curses are involved—enmity with humans for the snake, pain in childbirth for the woman, sweaty toil for the man. The ground itself is cursed on account of human error, producing thorns and thistles to go along with its red berries and purple flowers. The earthlings' short tenure in Eden comes to a sad and sudden end.

Distracted by such furious activity, many readers of this story have somehow gotten the idea that physical labor is part of God's curse—labor pains for the woman and field labor for the man—until labor itself gets all mixed up with punishment. Clearly, this is not so. The earthling's first divine job is to till the earth and keep it. If you have ever tilled a rose garden, much less a garden of Eden, then you know that this is difficult to do without getting sore shoulders. Keeping the earth is hard work. You get dirty doing it. You break fingernails and wear holes in the knees of your pants. You wear yourself out.

You also remember where you came from, and why. You touch the stuff your bones are made of. You handle the decomposed bodies of trees, leaves, birds, and fallen stars. Your body recognizes its kin. If you have nerve enough, you also foresee your own decomposition. This is not bad knowledge to have. It is the kind that puts other kinds in perspective. Feel that cool dampness? Welcome back to earth, you earthling. Smell that dirt? Welcome home, you beloved dust-creature of God.

While housework may not offer the same satisfaction, it remains a reliable path to the rudiments of life. Cleaning refrigerators and toilets helps you connect the food cycle at both ends. Making beds reminds you that life-giving activities do not require much space. Hanging laundry on the line offers you a chance to fly prayer flags disguised as bath towels and underwear. If all life is holy, then anything that sustains life has holy dimensions too. The difference between washing windows and resting in God can be a simple decision: choose the work, and it becomes your spiritual practice. Spraying vinegar and water on the panes, you baptize the glass. Rubbing away the film, ye repent ye of your sins. Polishing the glass, you let in the light. No task is too menial to serve as a path. If you are able to sustain other lives along with your own, then all the better.

Many years ago now, I volunteered at a city shelter for people with nowhere else to sleep. In the summertime, there were nights with vacant beds, but never in wintertime. The minute the temperature dipped below freezing, the line outside would stretch around the block. Regular volunteers rotated through all the jobs required to make the place go: checking people in, cooking and serving supper, keeping peace through the night, cleaning up in the morning. I was not a regular volunteer, but as a clergyperson at the host church I thought I should show up at least once a season.

On the night I am remembering I did a little bit of everything, including playing cards with the overnight guests. I slept in a chair, but only for a few hours. By 6:00 a.m., it was time to empty the place out so the volunteers could get to their regular jobs. The cleanup list included everything from stacking the mattresses to sweeping the floors. It is unclear to me how I ended up with the job of cleaning the toilets. Was it the clergy thing? Or was it because I only showed up once a season?

Whatever it was, the toilets were mine—all three of them—all smelling of vomit, all splattered with diarrhea, all slick with urine. Short of falling headfirst into a septic tank, I could not imagine anything worse, which made it the perfect job for me. Scrubbing the bowls one by one, I thought of Saint Francis kissing lepers. I thought of Jesus washing feet. I thought of Mother

Teresa bathing the dying of Calcutta. By the time I reached the third bowl I was entirely out of spiritual fantasies, which left me free to remember that I too used toilets, occasionally as these toilets had been used. I was made of the same stuff as other humans. What came out of me smelled no better than what came out of anyone else. Welcome back to earth, you earthling. Welcome home, you beloved dirt-person of God.

That was a morning to remember, but life offers no shortage of opportunities to engage physical labor. Sometimes the work comes attached to an ice storm, offering you little choice but to freeze or to cope. Other times it presents itself to you as drudgery, which you may turn into soul work by choosing the labor instead of resenting it. However the openings come to you, they offer you the chance to bear the reality of the universe in your flesh like a thorn. The difficulty, Simone Weil says, is to look upon them with love. Succeed at that, and you can be sure that what you love is Real, leading you deeper into the More that is your heart's desire.

10

The Practice of Feeling Pain

BREAKTHROUGH

There will come a time when you believe everything is
finished. That will be the beginning.
                              —*Louis L'Amour*

I had been teaching world religions for several years before I
realized how many of them grew out of suffering. Buddhism
began when the overprivileged Prince Siddhartha, protected from
suffering since his birth, left the palace grounds one day and saw
a sick man, an old man, and a dead man for the first time in his
life. These three passing sights so affected him that he dedicated
the rest of his life to easing the suffering of all who faced the pain
inherent in being alive.

Judaism's central story is the story of the Exodus, in which
God heard the cries of an immigrant people suffering forced
labor, fatal beatings, and the murder of their newborns in the

land of Egypt. Recruiting a royal fugitive named Moses to free them, God led them by pillars of fire and cloud through more suffering in the wilderness until they emerged a new people with a new future in a new land.

Christianity began when Jesus emerged from his own wilderness experience to minister to the suffering of an occupied people—occupied not only by Rome but also by the fear that their long oppression meant God had abandoned them. He addressed this fear by healing the sick, feeding the hungry, and freeing those who were possessed by demons, even though his care for other people's pain put him in grave risk of bringing pain upon himself. His death on a Roman cross became both the epitome of human suffering and the proof that even suffering such as that could not force one chosen by God to leave the path of love.

Islam began in a cave outside the desert city of Mecca, where the prophet Muhammad prayed to God for some solution to the tribal warfare that was tearing his people apart. When the angel Gabriel appeared on that Night of Power, commanding him to recite the first verses of the Qur'an, the Prophet had the beginning of God's answer. Years later, forced from the city of his birth under relentless persecution and threat of death, he led a small band of followers north to Yathrib, where these first Muslims found peace and welcome at last.

I could go on, but you get the idea. Pain is provocative. Pain pushes people to the edge, causing them to ask fundamental questions such as "Why is this happening?" and "How can this be fixed?" Pain brings out the best in people along with the worst. Pain strips away all the illusions required to maintain the status quo. Pain begs for change, and when those in its grip find no release on earth, plenty of them look to heaven—including some whose formal belief systems preclude such wishful thinking.

Since feeling pain is not optional for human beings, I have some explaining to do. How can something as nonnegotiable as feeling pain serve as a spiritual practice? Like all the other aspects of the human condition described in this book—from having a body and being with other people to doing work and needing rest—feeling pain is something else that can be handled in a variety of ways. I can try to avoid pain. I can deny pain. I can numb it and I can fight it. Or I can decide to engage pain when it comes to me, giving it my full attention so that it can teach me what I need to know about the Really Real.

If you have ever made a graph of your life—writing your birthday at the left side of a page and today's date at the right, filling in the major events that have made you who you are—then you are likely to note that the spikes in your pain bear some relationship to the leaps in your growth. It was when your family moved for the fourth time in five years that you learned to enjoy your own company in the months before you made new friends at school. It was when your partner left you that you remembered what else you meant to do in your life beyond staying together. It was when the doctor called about the spot on your lung that you finally made up with your sister. These are not the ways you would have chosen to become more than you were, but they worked. Pain burned up the cushions you used to keep from hitting bottom. Pain popped your clutch and shot you into the next gear. Pain landed you flat in bed, giving you time to notice things you never slowed down enough to notice before.

Pain makes theologians of us all. If you have spent even one night in real physical pain, then you know what that can do to your faith in God, not to mention your faith in your own ability to manage your life. One afternoon when I was pruning trees, I stuck a sharp stick in my right eye by mistake. It hurt badly enough right then that I dropped my pruning shears and staggered to the house to wash the pine bark out of my eye. An hour later, it hurt badly enough for me to ask my husband to drive me to the emergency room, where a physician's assistant put some numbing orange dye in my eye and said everything looked all right. An hour after that, when the numbness had worn off, I took a bunch of aspirin and went to bed, hoping to find some relief from the pain in my sleep.

Every time I woke up, the pain in my right eye shot through me like an electrical shock. Every time it did, I cried out loud. I took more aspirin and fell asleep again. I woke up and got shocked again. My right eye felt as if there were still a large chunk of pine bark in it, so I felt my way downstairs and lay down in the bathtub, letting warm water run from the faucet straight into my eye. The pain got worse, not better. While the grandfather clock in the dining room tolled hour after hour, I prayed the kind of prayers I never thought I would pray. I began the kind of bargaining with God that I do not even believe in, and when that did not work I called God's honor into question. I begged God to do something. I dared God to do something. Finally, close to dawn, I found myself turning away from the God in charge of pain removal toward the God who had stayed with me through the pain no matter what I said. By the time I saw an optometrist who told me I had a torn cornea, my midnight wrestling match was over. The pain had not only changed the way I prayed. It had also changed my ideas about the One to whom I prayed.

Pain is one of the fastest routes to a no-frills encounter with the Holy, and yet the majority of us do everything in our power to avoid it. We spend a great deal of money on painkillers. We drown our sorrows in alcohol. We ask for nitrous oxide at the dentist's office. The small circle of those who willingly choose pain both fascinate and appall us: people as different from one another as the women who bear children without anesthesia, the teenagers who cut themselves, the religious enthusiasts who whip themselves or dance lashed to trees by cords passed through the skin of their chests. While I know people who do all of these things, I am not equipped to write about them.[1] The only pain I know well is the garden variety, which easily fills all the baskets I have.

When I was in high school I feared needles so much that I decided I would never marry as long as a blood test was required. As best I can recall, this fear originated in a vaccination I received when I was four years old. By then I was big enough to fight the county nurse, who cursed audibly when I jerked away just as she plunged the needle into my right buttock. The needle broke off, which left her holding a spewing syringe as I fell to the floor and rolled under the examining table. I was dragged from my safe hole by several strong women in white. My mother may have been among them, although I have exonerated her so fully that I do not recall seeing her face as I was returned to custody. The needle was removed with a pair of pliers. The wound was swabbed with alcohol that smelled like liquid pain to me. I was pinned down for the second try at my vaccination, which was over before I had time to yell. I left the doctor's office a defeated but immunized child.

The trauma was such that I later refused Novocain when I went to the dentist's office as a teenager. This makes no sense, I know, but I feared the needle worse than I feared the drill, and no amount of reasoning on my dentist's part could change my mind. The pain was exquisite but bearable. It was like being stung by a wasp with a really long stinger for a really long time, while someone tapped on my jaw with a ball-peen hammer. The pain was very focusing. My mind did not wander at all. Plus, when it was over, it was over. My dentist looked worse than I did as I got up from the chair and thanked him for his work.

When it came time to have my wisdom teeth out, I caved in. I watched the orthodontist slide a tiny butterfly needle into a vein on the back of my hand, I started counting backward from ten, and the next thing I knew I was coming to with a mouth full of cotton wadding that smelled like iron. After that, I became a great fan of anesthesia. I asked for it every chance I got. Why feel pain if you do not have to? A needle is a small price to pay. I even got married, although I had to stay awake for the blood test.

Later, I learned that it is often harder to sit with someone in pain than it is to feel pain yourself. In the 1980s I sat with a lot of people dying of AIDS. It was a killer then. It also scared those who did not have it to death, so that people who were sick with AIDS were often lonely as well. When I went to see someone in the hospital, I had to stop at a cart by the door to his room and put on a gown, a surgical mask, and rubber gloves. I knew that this was for his protection, not mine, but it did not feel that way. It felt like I was insulating myself from him, making sure that his flesh never touched my flesh, when that was exactly what both of us needed.

Some of those young men never left the hospital. Others returned on a regular basis. In between I visited them at home, where we could forgo the white paper outfits and talk without masks. I learned at least two things about pain during all those years. One was that after a while there is no reason to talk about it. When pain is as ubiquitous as air, why comment on it? Better to go where the pain leads, down to the ground floor where all the real things are: real love, real sorrow, real thanks, real fear. After a tête-à-tête down there, you can lose your appetite for tabloid gossip and shopping news.

The second thing I learned is that there is a difference between pain and suffering, which I have used as synonymous until now. Pain, according to the American Medical Association, is "an unpleasant sensation related to tissue damage." That language is a little too restrained for the situations I have in mind, but it is scientifically correct. Pain originates in the body. The hurt comes from swollen joints, fluid-filled lungs, damaged nerves, invading tumors. More often than not, you can lay your hands on pain. You can find the place that hurts and press it, eliciting a howl or at least a grunt from the person it belongs to. Pain happens in the flesh.

Suffering, on the other hand, happens in the mind. The mind decides what pain means and whether it is deserved. The mind notices who comes to visit and who does not. The mind remembers how good things used to be and are not likely to be again. The mind makes judgments, measures loss, takes blame, and assigns guilt. In the case of my friends with AIDS, their suffering included parents who would not acknowledge their lovers, landlords who would not renew their leases, employers who would not hold their jobs, and insurance companies that would not care for their survivors. While there is no doubt it was AIDS that finally killed them, I think their suffering was often worse than their pain.

It is difficult to bear or even to be near either one without entertaining grave questions about divine justice. Theodicy is the oldest religious question in the book: if God is all-powerful and God is all-good, then why do terrible things happen to good people? How can God's reputation survive one child who dies before her sixth birthday, much less the death toll of an AIDS epidemic or a tsunami?

The biblical book of Job famously wrestles with this question without ever winning an answer from God. Along the way, it exposes most of the truth about pain along with most of the folly in traditional religious answers to it. That this book is in the Bible at all is a testament to those who decided to include it. Apparently they too recognized that an uncensored account of the depth of human pain and suffering is more to be valued than any correct doctrinal answer to it.

In the first place, there is no question that Job is good. He is a blameless and upright man who fears God and turns away from evil. Even God agrees with this assessment, which is why Satan chooses Job as a test case in faithfulness. Of course Job fears you, Satan says, since you have done nothing but bless him all his life. You have protected Job from harm, prospered his work, and given him everything his heart desires, including seven sons, three daughters, and something in the neighborhood of twelve thousand head of livestock. You have made Job a great man, the greatest in the East. If Job loves you, Satan suggests, then this love is not exactly what you would call unconditional. Hurt him, Satan says, hurt him bad, and he will curse you to your face.

This Satan is not the devil of popular religious imagination. Job is a book with one deity, not two. Here Satan is the "Accuser," God's prosecuting attorney, who serves among the heavenly beings on God's divine council. He has no power to operate independently of God. He can only do to Job what God gives him permission to do. So when Satan hurts Job, he does it with divine license—first by robbing Job of his livestock, then by causing a house to fall on his children, and finally by causing Job to be covered with festering boils from the soles of his feet to the crown of his head. God will not allow Satan to kill Job, raising the question of whether there is pain and suffering worse than death, but throughout his trial Job does not turn away from God.

He does, however, let loose with quite a lot of rhetoric. Job curses the day he was born. He defends the justice of his cause.

He tells God to go pick on someone God's own size. "Will you not look away from me for a while," Job rages, "let me alone until I swallow my spittle?"[2] If anyone has ever lacked the words to lodge a fluent complaint against the Almighty, the script is right there in the Bible. Job is one of pain's most eloquent poets.

This in itself is something of a marvel, since pain so often defies description. If you have ever tried to tell a doctor how the pain you are feeling feels, then you know the limits of language. It feels like a burning hot coal has been inserted right under your sternum. It feels like someone has pounded a railroad spike into your head. It feels like your skin is on fire, like your eye has a piece of pine bark in it, like your spine has been replaced by an electrical wire that short-circuits every time you move like *that*.

Metaphors are all you have, since there are no words to describe the pain directly. Pain is not real in the same way that a stone or a piece of broken glass is real. Even a physician who asks you to rate your pain on a scale from one to ten cannot know how your "ten" compares to her last patient's "ten." As painful as it is, pain cannot be communicated except by approximation, which means that any description of pain requires imagination.

According to Job, his pain is like being pierced by poisonous arrows.[3] It is like being crushed by a tempest,[4] like being broken in two, like being seized by the neck and dashed to pieces.[5] God has slashed open his kidneys and poured his gall on the ground.[6] Job's skin turns black and falls off his body; his bones burn with heat.[7] But this is no more than the approximation of his pain. Job's suffering surpasses it, as he asks God to explain what has happened to him and receives no answer.

"Why me?" That is all Job wants to know. His physical pain is beyond words. The losses he has suffered are unspeakable. Yet Job will not shut up. With nothing else to do and nothing left to protect, he uses every verbal tool he has to pound on God's door: curses, tears, insolence, sarcasm, humility, indignation, reason. What has happened to him has so assaulted his sense of himself before God that he is no longer sure who he is. Job can make no meaning of it. He is furthermore unable to force God to make meaning of it either.

Here, then, is another feature of pain, including the pain of suffering. At its worst, it can erase most of what you thought you knew about yourself. People who live with chronic pain usually know more about this than those who may reasonably look forward to feeling better soon. To live with pain on a daily basis is to be involved in a high-maintenance relationship. To make peace with the pain can require as much energy as fighting it. Things you once did without thinking—rising, dressing, eating, walking—now take concerted effort, if not paid help. Who is this person who cannot do such simple things? Who is this person who cannot help anyone, not even herself?

One night of real pain is enough to strip away your illusions about how strong you are, how brave, how patient and faithful. Who would have thought that a torn cornea could hurt all the way down to the heels of your feet? Who would have imagined that a really bad case of food poisoning could make you doubt the mercy of God? You do not need a torturer standing over you to recognize the direct link between pain and truth. Pain is so real that less-real things like who you thought you were and how you meant to act can vanish like drops of water flung on a hot stove. Your virtues can become as abstract as algebra, your beliefs as porous as clouds.

Job believed that he knew God. He believed he was a good man, blameless and upright. This was not haughty posturing on his part. He looked after his servants and his animals. He was a good husband to his wife. He prayed regularly for their children, making sacrifices to cover any sins they may have forgotten to cover for themselves. He believed that all of this pleased God, and that the good things he enjoyed were the tangible blessings of God.

When everything begins falling apart for Job, so does his sense of reality. He is not who he thought he was. The world does not work the way he thought it did. His family is not safe. His health is not sure. Perhaps God is not who Job thinks God is, either? The only thing that can save Job's faith from a major overhaul is an explanation from God. "Why?" he asks over and over again, without receiving so much as a clearing of the divine throat.

Thus Job suffers from God's silence, which hurts him worse than his boils, worse than his poverty, worse even than the death of his children. Without an answer, his life is meaningless. How does meaninglessness feel? It is like falling through outer space without an oxygen mask on. It is like being tied to your bed by a thousand cobwebs. It is like walking through a crowded shopping mall without ever touching anyone or being touched in return.

Job has three friends who mean to rescue him from this meaninglessness. One by one, they come to him with their traditional explanations for his pain and suffering. He must have done *something* wrong, Eliphaz says. God is always right, Bildad adds. Even if Job does not know what he has done wrong, Zophar says, God does. Job should just go ahead, say he is sorry, and let God apply the repentance wherever it is due.

As ancient as these arguments are, they are as existential as they are theological. Even a toddler who bumps her head on the corner of a coffee table may ask her mother between sobs what she has done wrong. Because the pain hurts, *something* must be wrong. If she can discover the cause, then perhaps the pain will end. If she cannot end it herself, then she may still be able to seek the help of someone more powerful than she who can make the pain stop. If saying she is sorry will speed the process, then she will by all means say so.

The sad hole in this logic is the illusion that pain can be controlled—if not by the self, then by the love or manipulation of some power greater than the self. Any parent who has sat through the night by a sick child's bed knows that this is not so. There is pain with no known cause, just as there is pain with no known cure. The parent's suffering can exceed the child's pain. In Job's case, the reader knows that Job is in a pinch between God and Satan, but Job does not know that. All Job knows is that the pain and suffering go on and on while God remains silent.

Job turns from his friends, who in any case are more invested in defending God than they are in defending him. He will not heed their pious counsel, any more than he will follow his wife's advice to curse God and die. Job will deal with God or he will deal with no one. If God will not answer him, then he will fill the air with his own furious poetry. This is how faith looks, sometimes: a blunt refusal to stop speaking into the divine silence.

In one of his thousands of love poems to God, the Sufi mystic poet Rumi takes up the case of a man who spent his nights calling out God's name until his lips grew sweet with praise. Then one night a cynic asked the man if he had ever heard anything back. Since he had no answer to that, the man stopped praying and drifted into a muddled sleep. Khidr, the guide of souls, came to him in a dream and asked him why he had stopped praying.

"Because I've never heard anything back," the man said.

"This longing you express *is* the return message," Khidr told him.

The grief you cry out from
draws you toward union.

Your pure sadness
that wants help
is the secret cup.

Listen to the moan of a dog for its master.
That whining is the connection.

There are love dogs
no one knows the names of.

Give your life
to be one of them.[8]

Job is one of God's longest-winded love dogs. For thirty-seven chapters he fills the air with his grief, saying things to God that would have made his grandmother faint dead away if she had ever heard him say them.

Let me have silence, and I will speak,
   and let come on me what may.
I will take my flesh in my teeth,
   and put my life in my hand.
See, he will kill me; I have no hope;
   but I will defend my ways to his face.[9]

Job has become swollen with grief. The enormity of his pain has made him huge in his own eyes, so that he suffers not only from his losses and from the silence of God but also from the self-centeredness that comes naturally to those in great pain. Why do the elderly spend so much time cataloguing the list of things that hurt? Because these deep aches and stinging pains are their constant companions, taking up so much space and requiring so much attention, it is often difficult for another living human being to break through their closed circle and find a seat. While Job's suffering may be extraordinary, his self-absorption is not. Pain can propel the hurting self to the center of the universe.

When God finally speaks—not, apparently, because Job has been irresistibly persuasive but because God cannot stand one more minute of his yammering—God does not give Job a single answer to any of the questions he has asked about what has happened to him and why. Instead, God asks Job forty-three questions in a row, beginning with "Who is this that darkens counsel by words without knowledge?"[10] and ending with "Shall a fault-finder contend with the Almighty?"[11]

All of the questions in between are patently unanswerable. No, Job was not there when God laid the foundations of the earth. No, he has not entered into the springs of the sea, or walked in the recesses of the deep. No, he cannot send forth lightning, number the clouds, or tilt the waterskins of the heavens, any more than he can satisfy the appetite of the young lions, provide for the ravens, or give the horse its might. No, Job cannot. No, Job has not. No, Job does not know.

When God pauses to take a breath, Job is as close to speechless as he has ever been. "See, I am of small account," he says to God, "what shall I answer you?" Then he lays his hand on his mouth. "I have spoken once, and I will not answer," he says between his fingers, but since this is Job he cannot restrain himself; "twice, but will proceed no further."[12]

Testing him, God asks Job twenty more questions in a row, but God's point has been made. Job is not God. His pain does not set him apart from other living creatures. If anything, it secures his communion with them. God cares enough about Job to show him things no human has ever seen, but this does not place Job at the center of God's universe. God has other things to do, some of them quite important. Job may watch, but only if he keeps quiet.

For reasons that are not entirely clear, Job is satisfied with this answer. He sounds frankly relieved to be put back in his place, savoring at least two of the magisterial things God has said to him enough to repeat them out loud. "I had heard of you by the hearing of the ear," he says by way of conclusion, "but now my eye sees you; therefore I despise myself, and repent in dust and ashes."[13]

That last line drives some readers crazy. In it, they hear the blaming of the victim, the bowing down of a beaten man before a bullying God. But Job does not look beaten to me. He looks like someone whose pain has broken through everything he thought he knew—about himself, about life, about God—to deliver him to a new threshold of being. Of course he despises himself! He has just received a blast of truest reality, which has made his limited, self-absorbed grieving look small by comparison. The dust and ashes are for burying that smaller life, beloved as it was, and stepping into the larger life he has just seen in God's face.

What Job says matches what I have heard other pioneers say. Like him, they have given up asking the question of *why* bad things happen to good people. They know that the real question is *when*. What do you do when pain and its attendant suffering finally show up at your door? How can breakdown become breakthrough? How does a love dog moan for its master?

I have to be careful here, or I will sound like one of Job's pious friends. No one who is not in pain is allowed to give advice to someone who is. The only reliable wisdom about pain comes from the mouths of those who suffer it, which is why it is so important to listen to them. That way, when our turn comes, the rest of us will not be clueless. We will recognize at least some of the territory and remember what those who went before us told us about what comes next.

I have sat by as many deathbeds as sickbeds in my life, and I have listened carefully. I have also watched what goes on in the room, including the complications I have brought to it myself. I have seen pain twist people and those who love them into exhausted rags with all the hope squeezed out of them. I have also seen people in whom pain seems to have burned away everything extra, everything trivial, everything petty and less than noble, until they have become see-through with light. I wish I knew what accounted for the difference between the two, but coming up with a formula would be disrespectful of everyone involved.

Generosity seems to help. When my friend Matilda lost her voice to Lou Gehrig's disease, she took up watercolors. The walls of her kitchen were papered with paintings of fleshy flowers that Georgia O'Keeffe would have coveted. You could not visit Matilda without getting a paintbrush stuck in your own hand too. She did not care whether you felt like painting or not. Colors had become her language. If you wanted to communicate with Matilda, you spoke purple, you spoke fuchsia, you spoke mauve. When you were through with your grade-school version of a Johnny-jump-up, she would clap her hands and honk like a trumpeter swan.

When Pat could no longer rise from her bed, she asked for her jewelry box to be set beside her. If you did not find something you liked in there, then she would send you to her closet to choose a sweater or a blouse. She worked hard to give everything away before she died, but people kept bringing her new things to replace those she had dispatched. When someone gave her a polished stone with a hole in it to wear around her neck, she did not know what to make of it at first. "What is it?" she breathed, turning it around and around in front of her face. Then she brought it close to one eye so that she could look straight through the round middle of the stone. "Ah," she said, "now I see. This is the way through."

Rituals seem to help too. When Lucy was dying way before her time, the members of her house church gathered on her porch at night, singing hymns that she could hear through the windows of her bedroom. They covered her whole house with prayers, so that you could almost see them floating over the roof like a luminous silk parachute. I do not know whether the hymns helped Lucy, but I know they helped the people who sang them.

When Earl was facing his second cancer surgery, he was not sure how to prepare. He was not a churchgoer, having burned out on God during a painful childhood in parochial school. Like Thoreau, he preferred to go to the woods alone, but his illness made that difficult to do. So he sat in a spot of sunlight in his office instead, straightening his papers so no one would have a hard time finding things while he was gone. When two of his grown children found him there on the day before his surgery, they asked if they could lay hands on him.

Unable to think of a polite way to say no, he let them, holding very still as one of them laid both hands on his hot, round head, and the other pressed down on both of his shoulders hard enough for him to know how heavy love could be. The three of them stayed that way for what was either a long time or no time at all. In that posture, it was hard to tell. Nothing was said, during or after. It was only years later that Earl would bring it up, saying, "Remember that day you touched me in the sunlight? I still re-member that day."

Paying attention also helps: just that, just paying attention to the pain. Pain can hurt so badly that it begs a reason, causing people to drum up all sorts of guilt and debt to go with it. Even those who may be on the right track will never get the proportions right, so I wish they would just give it up. Better they should stop doing the math and take a look around, since they may never see as clearly as they do when pain clears their sight.

Plato once said that pain restores order to the soul. Rumi said that it lops off the branches of indifference. "The throbbing vein / will take you further / than any thinking."[14] Whatever else it does, pain offers an experience of being human that is as elemental as birth, orgasm, love, and death. Because it is so real, pain is an available antidote to unreality—not the medicine you would have chosen, perhaps, but an effective one all the same. The next time you are in real pain, see how you feel about television shows, new appliances, a clean house, or your resumé. Chances are that none of these will do anything for you. All that will do anything for you is some cool water, held out by someone who has stopped everything else in order to look after you. An extra blanket might also help, a dry pillow, the simple knowledge that there is someone in the house who might hear you if you cried.

Once, when I was confined to bed for the better part of a week, I spent hours watching the sunlight that came through the slats of my wooden blinds move down the white wall of my bedroom. First thing in the morning it made honey-colored rectangles with soft edges. By 10:00 a.m. the wall was striped with bands of light as straight as rulers. By noon they looked more like the rungs of a ladder, dappled with leaves from the winged elm outside my window. By 2:00 they had lost most of their character, as the sun moved over the roof of the house and left the front yard in deepening shadow.

This may sound boring to you, but it was not. It was beautiful. It was reassuring. It gave me a place outside myself to go. I did not have to do anything to make the light change. It had a routine it followed all by itself whether I was awake to watch it or not. If I did not like the way the light looked at a given moment, I knew it would change. If I loved the way the light looked at a given moment, I knew it would change. I could not speed it up and I could not slow it down. Not to put too fine a point on it, the light was my life and I knew it. Paying attention to it, I lost my will to control it. Watching it, I became patient. Letting it be, I became well.

There will always be people who run from every kind of pain and suffering, just as there will always be religions that promise to put them to sleep. For those willing to stay awake, pain remains a reliable altar in the world, a place to discover that a life can be as full of meaning as it is of hurt. The two have never canceled each other out and I doubt they ever will, at least not until each of us—or all of us together—find the way through.

11

The Practice of Being Present to God

PRAYER

> The best preparation for a life of prayer is to become more intensely human.
>
> —*Kenneth Leech*

I know that a chapter on prayer belongs in this book, but I dread writing it. I have shelves full of prayer books and books on prayer. I have file drawers full of notes from courses I have taught and taken on prayer. I have meditation benches I have used twice, prayer mantras I have intoned for as long as a week, notebooks with column after column of the names of people in need of prayer (is writing them down enough?). I have a bowed psaltery—a biblical stringed instrument mentioned in the book of Psalms—that dates from the year I thought I might be able to sing prayers easier than I could say them. I have invested a small fortune in icons, candles, monastic incense, coals, and incense burners.

I am a failure at prayer. When people ask me about my prayer life, I feel like a bulimic must feel when people ask about her favorite dish. My mind starts scrambling for ways to hide my problem. I start talking about other things I do that I hope will make me sound like a godly person. I try to say admiring things *about* prayer so there can be no doubt about how important I think it is. I ask the other person to tell me about *her* prayer life, hoping she will not notice that I have changed the subject.

I would rather show someone my checkbook stubs than talk about my prayer life. I would rather confess that I am a rotten godmother, that I struggle with my weight, that I fear I am overly fond of Bombay Sapphire gin martinis than confess that I am a prayer-weakling. To say I love God but I do not pray much is like saying I love life but I do not breathe much. The only way I have found to survive my shame is to come at the problem from both sides, exploring two distinct possibilities: 1) that prayer is more than my idea of prayer and 2) that some of what I actually do in my life may constitute genuine prayer.

Two monks have been great helps to me in these explorations. The first is Brother David Steindl-Rast, an Austrian Benedictine who joined a monastery in New York while I was still in diapers. Years later he wrote a book called *gratefulness, the heart of prayer,* which Henri Nouwen required in his courses at Yale Divinity School. Unlike many of the books I read in seminary, this one was not complicated. Even Brother David said that it could be summarized in two words: Wake up! Borrowing the words of the poet Kabir, he explained what he meant:

Do you have a body? Don't sit on the porch!
Go out and walk in the rain!
If you are in love,

then why are you asleep?
Wake up, wake up!
You have slept millions and millions of years.
Why not wake up this morning? [1]

This was the first inkling I had that prayer might mean something more than getting down on my knees, either in public or in private, to address God in a way that was respectful enough, focused enough, unselfish and theologically correct enough to merit God giving up some time to listen. By then I had studied the Catechism in the back of the Book of Common Prayer, discovering that there were seven different kinds of prayers: adoration, praise, thanksgiving, penitence, oblation, intercession, and petition. My difficulty was that I could not keep them straight.

When I prayed for people I loved who were sick, was that intercession or petition? When I thanked God for the beauty of the earth, was that praise or thanksgiving? It reminded me of the days when I entered sermon contests, reading the descriptions of the prize categories over and over again in order to decide where my sermon belonged. Was it a topical sermon or an expository one? Was it a pastoral sermon or a prophetic one? I could never decide, any more than I could produce a sermon that fit into one of those boxes without flopping over the sides.

In spite of my difficulty with the categories, I learned that prayer was not a contest. The categories in the prayer book were for sharpening my intention, not for winning God's attention. How then should I pray? When I fretted over people I knew who were in trouble, so that my worry for them followed me around all day like a hungry dog, was that prayer? When I cooked dinner for people who had plenty to eat at home, thinking about them while I chopped the turnip greens and mashed the sweet potatoes, was that prayer? When I went outside after everyone had gone to bed and moaned at the moon because I could not come up with the right words to say what was in my heart, was that prayer?

Brother David was the first person to tell me that prayer is not the same thing as prayers. Prayers are important, he said. Saying psalms in the morning is a good way to head into the day more prayerfully. So is going to church, where I can add my voice to those of a whole congregation aiming to woo God's ears with their ancient, beautiful cadences. Still, prayer is more than saying set prayers at set times. Prayer, according to Brother David, is waking up to the presence of God no matter where I am or what I am doing. When I am fully alert to whatever or whoever is right in front of me; when I am electrically aware of the tremendous gift of being alive; when I am able to give myself wholly to the moment I am in, then I am in prayer. Prayer is happening, and it is not necessarily something that I am doing. God is happening, and I am lucky enough to know that I am in The Midst.

When Brother David said that even biting into a tomato can be a kind of prayer, he had me. Anyone who recognizes the sacramental value of a homegrown tomato sandwich can be my spiritual director. He also gave me the bridge to my other monk, Nicholas Herman, who lived more than three hundred years ago in France. Herman served as a soldier and then as a footman to the treasurer of the king of France before something led him to the kitchen of a Discalced ("Shoeless") Carmelite monastery in Paris when he was thirty-eight years old. The Carmelites took Herman in and he became a lay brother, working as "a servant of the servants of God" for the rest of his life. Better known as Brother Lawrence, he left a cache of notes and letters behind that his abbot, Joseph de Beaufort, published after his death, knowing full well how much this would have embarrassed Brother Lawrence.

"I am writing only under the condition that you will not share my letter with anyone," he confided to a nun who wrote him for advice. "If I knew that you were to let it be seen, all the desire I have for your perfection would not be able to persuade me to do it."[2]

But he did do it, and his abbot did publish it, in a volume called *The Practice of the Presence of God*, which has become a spiritual classic. This is ironic, since Brother Lawrence readily admitted that books on the spiritual life served only to confuse him. He was also no good at set prayers. While he dutifully completed the three hours of prayer and meditation required of the monks in his order each day, he confessed that afterward he could not have said what it had all been about.

Once, he wrote, he met a very devoted woman who told him that the spiritual life "is a life of grace that begins with servile fear, increases through the hope of eternal life, and is consummated by pure love. She also insisted that people have different degrees by which they finally arrive at this happy consummation."

"I have not followed any of these methods," Brother Lawrence admitted. "On the contrary, for reasons I do not understand, they made me afraid at first." Instead, he resolved to give himself wholly to God no matter what he was doing, "and out of love for Him to renounce everything that was not Himself."[3]

Fortunately for the monks he served, this did not mean renouncing the pancakes that he made for them, the wine he bought for them, or the shoes he cobbled for them. Having resolved to do all of these things and more while keeping his attention focused lovingly on God, Brother Lawrence discovered such joy "that in order to restrain it and keep from revealing it, I am forced into childish actions that appear more like madness than devotion."[4] If he dared use the term, he said, he would call this state of joy being nursed by God, for the indescribable sweetness that he experienced at God's breast.

Of course he also experienced the aches and pains of incarnation, including sciatica, gout, and pleurisy. Like Brother David, Brother Lawrence was not innocent of pain or suffering. He knew as much about the sorrowful mysteries of God as he did about the joyful ones. He would have understood what Brother David meant when he wrote, "pain is a small price to pay for freedom from self-deception."[5]

If I am attached to both of these monks, it is because neither of them needs me to be a monk too. It is fine with them for me to teach school, go to the grocery store, clean the cat litter pan, and do the laundry. It is fine with them for me to know far more spiritual methods than I use and to say the Lord's Prayer without really thinking about every word. It is even fine with them for me to think I am a failure at prayer as long as I go on nudging at God's breast, letting the smell of that sweet milk lead me deeper into the ordinary activities of my every day.

When I look up from feeding the outside dogs to see the full moon coming up through the bare trees like the wide iris of God's own eye—when I feel the beam of it enter my busy heart straight through the zipper of my fleece jacket and fill me full of light—I am in prayer. When I spend all afternoon chopping onions, stewing tomatoes, and setting the dining room table with every piece of silver I own for a supper of soup and bread with friends, I am in prayer. When I am so sick that I cannot do anything but lie in bed with a jar of Vick's Vaporub and a blister pack of cold pills lost somewhere in the sheets, with all the time in the world to remember whom I love and why, I am in prayer.

This enlarged awareness answers none of the difficult questions about set prayers. Does prayer work or doesn't it? Never mind for a moment how many different things "work" might mean. Is it right for me to ask God for particular outcomes, when God alone knows what is right? Isn't the point of prayers to sharpen my hearing, not God's? Are words necessary at all? Is emptying the mind of all thought a surer path to God than trying to turn my thoughts to God? The only way to answer such questions is to engage a long-term habit of prayer. The virtue of such practice is that the questions change as the practice deepens, and no two people travel the exact same route.

Still, there are some predictable crises along the way. For instance, I do not know anyone who prays very long without running into the wall of God's apparent nonresponsiveness. There are probably adults of real faith in the world who pray without ever thinking about results, but I do not know any of them. Most of the people I know hunger for some evidence that God hears their prayers. Plenty of them would settle for a divine "no" as long as it was a clear one. The rest cling to the biblical promise that God will not give a snake to someone who asks for a fish, any more than God will give a stone to someone who asks for bread.

"If you ask anything in my name, I will do it," Jesus says in the gospel of John, leaving a lot of us wondering what it is about "in my name" that we do not understand.

Years ago now a brilliant friend of mine, a teacher in a big university, did everything in his power to ease the suffering of his lover, who was dying. Since that is his story to tell, not mine, all

I will say here is that one afternoon near the end I listened to the rawness of his prayers—pleading with God to do something, to work a miracle that would save his partner's life—and when the time was right I asked him to tell me about those prayers.

"You want to know whether I really believe God will intervene like that?" I think he asked me. "You wonder if I am really that naïve?" Then he told me something that I once knew but had long forgotten, although thanks to him I am not likely to forget again.

"Honestly," he said, "I don't think it through, not now. I tell God what I want. I'm not smart enough or strong enough to do anything else, and besides, there's no time. So I tell God what I want and I trust God to sort it out." Maybe that is what Jesus meant about coming to God like a child. The Ph.D. in prayer is optional.

I do not know any way to talk about answered prayer without sounding like a huckster or a honeymooner. When someone wants to tell me how God has answered prayer, those are the first two possibilities that occur to me, anyway: 1) This person wants to sell me something, or 2) This person is not quite sober yet. The problem, I think, is that divine response to prayer is one of those beauties that remain in the eye of the beholder. What sounds like an answer to one person sounds like silence to another. What seems like a providentially big fish to someone registers as blind luck for someone else. The meaning we give to what happens in our lives is our final, inviolable freedom. Only you can say whether God answered you. If you have any sense, you will ask someone with more experience than you to help you decide what the answer means, but even then the choice is yours. Are you still waiting for God to answer you, or is your life the answer you have been seeking, hiding in plain view?

•   •   •

WAITING IS CERTAINLY a kind of prayer, especially if you can stand howling, wide-open spaces. Once, between the time my doctor gave me some bad news about my health and the time I was scheduled for surgery to have the bad thing cut out, I found it possible to love my life in ways that had never occurred to me before. I never thought I could value being able to walk around my house and look out all the windows. I never thought of the brickwork on the building where I worked as beautiful before, or the sound of people laughing on the sidewalk outside as welcome signs of life. I never allowed myself the time to take a bath instead of a shower, or to find out how long the hot water lasted if I were not in a hurry. Waiting, I found speechless intimacy with other people who were living in such wide-open spaces themselves. We lived in a whole different world from those who thought they were fine. We could spend fifteen minutes admiring a rose, a whole hour enjoying a meal. Even if my news had stayed bad instead of getting better, I like to think that these simple pleasures would not have lost their power to console me. They constituted an answer to my prayer for more life, even if that life turned out to be shorter than the one I thought I wanted.

The same thing can happen while you are waiting to learn whether your child will come home, whether your marriage will last, whether the war will end, whether the market will recover. If uncertainties like these are the sort that move people to pray, then that is because they are the ones that remind us how little real sway we have. Our lives are inextricably bound up with the lives of other people. So much depends on things we can never control. A butterfly beats its wings in Beijing, making it impossible to predict the weather in New York.

We are players, but we do not direct the play. Crucial decisions were made for us before we were even born. Did you decide to be born in Wichita? Was being a girl your first choice? Did you plan on growing up with three brothers, or none, to one parent or two? Even the decisions we make for ourselves seldom take us where we meant to go. I meant to stay married to the same person all my life. I meant to leave the South. I meant to give myself to the service of God until all my sharp edges were worn away.

None of those things happened. Other things happened instead, many of them against my will. Some of them turned out better than I could have planned and others of them much worse. So far there is nothing that I would make un-happen, if that were within my power. While I pray daily to be delivered from the most awful things that can happen to human beings—land mines, wasting illness, killing poverty, civil wars—I give thanks for even the semi-terrible things that have happened to me, since they have shown me what is really real. They have made me tell the truth. They have quashed all my illusions of control, leaving me with no alternative but to receive my life as an unmitigated gift.

In the same way that I am willing to thank my husband for a gift even before I have opened it—because I know him, because I trust his love of me, because I have faith we will survive even if he has given me a pneumatic nail gun for my birthday—I am willing to thank God for my life even before I know how it turns out. This is brave talk, I know, while I can still pay the bills, walk without assistance, and talk someone into going to the movies with me. My hope is that if I can practice saying thank you now, when I still approve of most of what is happening to me, then perhaps that practice will have become habit by the time I do not like much of anything that is happening to me. The plan is to replace approval with gratitude. The plan is to take what *is* as God's ongoing answer to me.

Within that widened frame, I stay curious about all the different ways there are to pray set prayers, since those particular practices strike me as the stitches that keep the quilt of prayer in place. Because I teach world religions—and because I take students on lots of field trips—we have rich opportunities to pray with a wide variety of people in their home settings.

When we visit the Vedanta Center for weekday vespers, we join the Swami in a few simple verses and then we sit quietly on cushions for close to an hour, focusing all of our attention on listening to God instead of trying to get God to listen to us. This is the longest that some of us have ever intentionally remained silent, which means that it is also the first time some of us have found the entrance to the vast wilderness inside. Young people whose heads stay full of iTunes, Spanish homework, instant messaging, play practice, parental advice, Guitar Hero, cross-country, term papers, e-mail, romantic sagas, *CSI*, chorale, X Box, debate team, Second Life, baseball, and the procurement of illegal substances can be startled to hear the sound of their own heartbeats for the first time. They had no idea there was so much space inside of them. No one ever taught them how to hold still enough long enough for the shy deer-soul inside of them to step into the clearing and speak.

When we visit the Greek Orthodox cathedral for the Divine Liturgy on Sunday morning, we stand for almost two hours, our minds coasting through the largely Greek service as we watch the morning light play across the golden icons, the floor-to-ceiling mosaics, the gilded doors to the high altar, where the priest blesses the sacred bread and wine in a hushed voice we are not meant to hear. Every now and then one of us has the strong sense that someone is looking at us, although no one around us is paying us any attention. Finally someone looks up to see the giant eyes of Christ the Pantocrator beaming down on all our heads from the heavenly dome of the ceiling. The students begin elbowing one another, all down the pew, until we are sitting with our heads bent back like people lying on the grass watching fireworks. Christ's head is huge. All twelve of us could fit inside it, if only we could figure out some way to get up there.

Not knowing the language turns out to be a kind of blessing. We can listen to the music without worrying about the words. We can let the prayers wash over us without analyzing their content. Since we do not understand what the priest is saying, we can watch what he is doing. We can see the reverent gestures going on all around us without being certain what they mean. When the long service is finally over, we are invited up to the altar for pieces of blessed bread. The priest knows we are not Orthodox and still he beckons us to come. We do not kiss his ring as some of the people ahead of us do, but he smiles at us all the same. The crusty bread he puts in our hands is white and yeasty. I chew mine all the way back to my pew.

When we go to the Reform synagogue for a Shabbat morning prayer service, it is one of those rare Saturdays when no bar or bat mitzvah is scheduled to take place. This means that we outnumber the congregants, who nod and smile at us as they take their seats. We have made sure to sit far enough back that we are not in anyone's regular pew. We also want to get a good view. Soon the rabbi enters along with the cantor. Both are women with dark hair and radiant smiles. Both wear elegant kippahs and prayer shawls. When the cantor begins to sing, the congregation sings with her. We find the words in the prayer book but not the music.

Everyone but us knows the music by heart. This sets us just far enough outside the circle of prayer to notice what is happening inside of it. The people are intent on their prayers, not one another. Some sing with their eyes closed, while others point out the Hebrew for their children.

When the rabbi gets ready to read the Torah portion for the day, she looks up at us. "Come stand with me while I read," she says. We turn around to see if she is speaking to someone behind us, but there is no one behind us. She is inviting us forward for the reading of the Torah. Although none of us knows what to do or how to behave once we are up there, we instinctively understand that this is not an invitation to which one says no. So we go—all of us, with our uncovered heads, in our too-skimpy clothes, at least one of us with a big rhinestone cross around her neck—to stand with the rabbi for the reading of God's holy word.

Once we are there, we huddle around her, holding our hands in front of our laps like we are posing for a school picture. We smile nervously at the members of the congregation whom we outnumber. Then the cantor points at a Hebrew word on the page with a little golden pointer shaped like a hand and the rabbi begins to chant. I can see over her shoulder since I am at least four inches taller than she is. Her glistening black hair smells like shampoo. Her voice is husky and resonant. I do not know what she is saying but the words go straight to my heart. Maybe it is the way she is singing them that goes straight to my heart. Either way, I am deeply moved, and I think I am not alone. Back in the college van, one of the students says, "I felt at home there. I thought I would feel strange, but I didn't. I felt right at home."

When we go to the Muslim masjid, it takes longer to get comfortable. This is because most of us have heard nothing but terrible things about Islam. At the movies, Arabs have replaced

African-Americans as the villains of choice. Christian evangelists of record have called Muhammad a terrorist and a child molester. The only time we hear the call to prayer is in the background on the news, as a reporter covers the latest bombing in the Middle East. No wonder students are scared when we go to the masjid.

The largely African-American congregation we visit meets in a prayer hall that was once a supermarket. The men and women pray in the same room, which is why I go there. I have visited masjids where the women sit in damp basements listening to the imam over blown loudspeakers. At this one, the women sit in the back, with no screens or curtains separating them from the rest of the congregation. I thought I would mind sitting back there, at least until I sat there—with the grandmothers behind me on folding chairs, children lying in their mothers' laps all around me, and women in beautiful headscarves sitting so close to me that I could feel their body heat. Once I sat there, no one could have persuaded me to move. I had the best seat in the house.

Sitting on the floor has all kinds of virtues. In the first place, it is a great equalizer. When everyone is on the ground, no one's seat is higher than anyone else's. Everyone's three square feet of tan carpet look pretty much the same. In the second place, you get to take your shoes off. Whether this leaves you in sock feet, stocking feet, or bare feet, it goes a long way toward helping you relax. It also reminds you that you are on holy ground. No matter where you are sitting, you are probably sitting where someone has bent her head to the ground in prayer. This is probably true of the rest of the world as well, but at least in the prayer hall you are aware of it. In the third place, you may sit any way you want. You do not have to sit up straight and keep your feet on the floor. You may sit in the lotus position if you like, as long as you do not distract your neighbor.

Your neighbor may distract you, however, since her prayers are not interior phenomena. They involve her entire body, from the top of her forehead to the bottom of her rosy feet. After you have watched ten or twelve women pray, you begin to get the sequence: stand facing the direction of Mecca with your hands behind your ears; move your hands to meet at the center of your body; bend at the waist once, then again, then kneel until your forehead touches the floor; sit back on your heels with your hands on your knees; bend forward again; stand up; repeat the sequence all over again.

I heard one Muslim woman say how hard this was for her at first—not because she was out of shape but because it was hard for her to bow before anyone, even God. It had taken her a long time to get her feet under her, she said. It had taken her a long time to stand up for herself. To be asked to bow down before God—not just once or twice but five times every day—required her to surrender some things she had worked very hard to possess.

Listening to her, I decided I had to try it. I did not try to learn the spoken prayers that went with the motions. I just did the motions, ending up with my nose buried in the carpet in my bedroom and my butt up in the air. Any words I had to say to God became entirely optional at that point. My posture said it all. My heart bowed before God. My brains bowed before God. My bowels and lungs bowed before God. I could not see anything but the carpet. I could not feel anything but my sorry knee joints. I could not hear anything but my own labored breathing echoing back up at me. I was not just in prayer; I was under prayer, entirely submerged in the act of surrendering my whole self to God.

The next time I was at the masjid, I stepped aside at the end of jumma prayers, when the whole congregation stands up in perfectly straight lines to make their final prostrations. I stood aside because I was not sure I could get through the whole sequence without messing up. I stood aside because I did not know what my students would think of me if I tried. I stood aside because I am not a Muslim, but when the six hundred people in that room all bent down before God in such perfect unison that a breeze swept the fine hairs away from my face, I felt the prayer in my body. Without moving a muscle, I felt my bones bend in surrender to almighty God.

All of these visits have aided my sense that there are real things I can do, both in my body and in my mind, to put myself in the presence of God. God is not obliged to show up, but if God does, then I will be ready. At the same time, I am aware that prayer is more than something I do. The longer I practice prayer, the more I think it is something that is always happening, like a radio wave that carries music through the air whether I tune in to it or not. This is hard to talk about, which is why prayer is a practice and not a discussion topic. The best I can do is to tell you how it works for me.

Since I am a failure at prayer, I keep an altar in my room. It is really an old vanity made of rosewood, with fancy scrollwork around the oval mirror and a small stack of drawers on either side. At worst, I think of it as a piece of furniture that I offer God as a substitute for my prayers. At best, I think of it as a portal that stays open whether I go through it or not. I keep some icons on it, and a lot of candles. When people ask me to pray for them, I write their names on slips of paper and put them in a small brass box that sits in front of two paintings, one of Jesus and one of his mother. Although Mary is looking lovingly in her son's direction, she occupies her own space, which I like.

Mary is more like me than her son is, after all. Both of her parents were human. She was born and she died in the usual ways. What was unusual about her was her reliability. No matter what life pitched at her, Mary did not duck. She endured a difficult pregnancy to bear a singular child, whom she loved reliably through all the years of his controversial life. When her son was cut down, she was there. When it came time to prepare his body, she was there. When he was not in his tomb, she was there. As much as I hate to presume on her reliability, I know she will remember the people whose names I have placed in the brass box, even when I forget.

Most nights the altar just sits there, holding all of those pictures, wicks, and names. Then comes a night when I am in deep need, deep fear, deep thanks, or deep want—either for myself or for someone I love—and I light every candle on the altar. Some are tall and thin. Others are short and squat. Some smell like vanilla and others like sandarac balsam. Some were gifts. I bought others for myself. Lighting them all generally requires at least ten kitchen matches, and even then I burn myself getting to the last of them. When I am through, I sit back on my heels and try to take it all in. The mirror behind the candles doubles their glow. The icons catch the light, pitching it back and forth. I can see my reflection through the flames, though only dimly, since the mirror is an old one that has lost much of its shine.

Prayer overtakes me there. I am utterly swamped by the presence of the Holy. I would bend my head to the ground if I could take my eyes off the beauty. As it is, I do not even know for sure if I am breathing. The altar is giving me more life than I know how to ask for. I can no longer tell the difference between need, fear, thanks, and want. In this light, I see how they are all facets of the same sparkler. I see how they are all faces of the same love. This answer to my prayer is so far beyond my doing that I cannot find the words to forswear my own input.

All I did was light the candles.
Did God find me or did I find God?
Hush.
The time for words is past.

12

The Practice of Pronouncing Blessings

BENEDICTION

> It is forbidden to taste of the pleasures of this world
> without a blessing.
>
> —*The Talmud*

As someone who has been paid to pronounce blessings at weddings and funerals, at baptisms and house blessings, at soup kitchens and foxhunts—as well as at lots and lots of weekly worship services—I think it is a big mistake to perpetuate the illusion that only certain people can bless things. Not everyone is vulnerable to this illusion, I know. Plenty of people say grace over meals in their own homes, asking God to bless the food they are about to receive from the divine bounty. A number more bless their children at bedtime, asking God to bring those children safely through the night. Where I live, you can sneeze in line at the post office and receive half a dozen blessings from people you do not even know.

Yet there remain a great many people who excuse themselves when asked to pronounce a formal blessing. They are not qualified, they say. They are not good with words. They would rather jump off a high diving board than try to say something holy in front of a bunch of other people. My guess is that even if you asked them to bless something in private—thereby separating the fear of public speaking from the fear of pronouncing a blessing—they would still demur. If you are one of those people, then only you know why. All I can tell you is how much the world needs you to reconsider.

When you are paid to pronounce blessings, you think about why that is, as well as about what is involved. Where did you get the idea you could do this? Is your job to confer holiness or to recognize it? Which things do you agree to bless and which things do you decline to bless? On what grounds do you decide which is which?

Different religious traditions offer different answers to these questions. Some reserve the blessing function for God alone. Others teach that a human blessing is the only kind there is. Since this is a book about practices and not a book about ideas, I think that the best way to discover what pronouncing blessings is all about is to pronounce a few. The practice itself will teach you what you need to know.

Start with anything you like. Even a stick lying on the ground will do. The first thing to do is to pay attention to it. Did you make the stick? No, you did not. The stick has its own story. If you have the time to figure out what kind of tree it came from, that would be a start to showing the stick some respect. It is only "a stick" in the same way that you are "a human," after all. There is more to both of you than that. Is it on the ground because it is old or because it suffered mishap? Has it been lying there for a long time or did it just land? Is it fat enough for you to see its growth rings?

If you look at the stick long enough, you are bound to begin making it a character in your own story. It will begin to remind you of someone you know, or a piece of furniture you once saw in a craft co-op. There is nothing wrong with these associations, except that they take you away from the stick and back to yourself. To pronounce a blessing on something, it is important to see it as it is. What purpose did this stick serve? Did a bird sit on it? Did it bear leaves that sheltered the ground from the hottest summer sun?

At the very least, it participated in the deep mystery of drawing water from the ground, defying the law of gravity to deliver moisture to its leaves. How does a stick do that, especially one this size? Smell it. Is the scent of sap still there? This is no less than the artery of a tree that you are holding in your hand. Its tissue has come from the sun and from the earth. Put it back where you found it and it will turn back into earth again. Dust to dust and ashes to ashes. Will you say a blessing first? No one can hear you, so you may say whatever you like.

"Bless you, stick, for being you."

"Blessed are you, o stick, for turning dirt and sun into wood."

"Blessed are you, Lord God, for using this stick to stop me in my tracks."

I once asked a class of graduate students to read a book of poems by Wendell Berry called *A Timbered Choir*. The poems chronicle almost twenty years of Berry's walks through the woods on Sunday mornings. He calls them "The Sabbath Poems," which is a good thing to call them since they are as full of reverence as any worship service. Mostly he just pays attention to the things he sees: trees, fields, warblers, light. As he does, they become doors to other things: grief, love, amazement, blessing.

Reading him, you come gradually to understand that the key to blessing things is knowing that they beat you to it. The key to blessing things is to receive their blessing. You do not always have to use the magic words, either. Sometimes it is enough to see the world through a tree's eyes.

> What do the tall trees say
> To the late havocs in the sky?
> They sigh.
> The air moves, and they sway.
> When the breeze on the hill
> Is still, then they stand still.
> They wait.
> They have no fear. Their fate
> Is faith. Birdsong
> Is all they've wanted, all along.[1]

Since the graduate students to whom I assigned this book were students of ministry, a few no doubt wondered why they were reading poems about trees. I was thankful that Berry had used the word "Sabbath" in his title to help justify my choice. At the beginning of class I invited volunteers to read their favorite poems out loud to the rest of the class. That worked all right. The others listened respectfully, some of them closing their eyes and some of them looking like they were holding thermometers in their mouths.

By my count, at least half of them were ready to get to the prose part of the class. They had paid good money for tuition. It was not easy for them to get time off from their churches. They wanted something they could take notes on, sooner rather than later. So I stopped the poetry reading earlier than I had planned, but at the break I asked them all to go outside and read at least one poem to a tree. I could not have asked anyone to do something like that when I was thirty years old, but at fifty-six I am willing to take more risks. Some of the students looked at me as if they were deciding whether it was too late to transfer to another class, but most of them took their Berry books with them when they left the room.

After the break, I had some converts.

"I read those poems before I got here," one of them said, "and they were okay. Poetry's just not my thing. But when I read one of them to the tree like you said, it sounded different to me. It was like the words had an inside and an outside and I had only read the outside. Reading them to the tree, I heard the inside. The words were so beautiful I almost cried."

"I felt completely stupid," another one said, "standing there in the quadrangle reading to a tree, but after a couple of lines I realized that the tree was really liking it. I am going to try reading to a bird next."

After the testimonials were over we all agreed that we would not speak to the other graduate students about this experience, at least not until happy hour. My point is how often we are embarrassed to do and say the things that really affect us. Perhaps this is because we cannot defend ourselves while they are happening. Or perhaps we have a corporate agreement that we will not embarrass one another, even if that means never going very deeply into the things that matter most to us.

If you are someone who does not like to start from scratch, you may want to learn about the Jewish tradition of *brakoth* before you start pronouncing blessings on your own. In Hebrew, a blessing prayer is a *brakha*. *Brakoth* is the plural form of the word, entirely necessary since an observant Jew says at least a hundred blessing prayers each day. There are prayers to be said upon waking up in the morning, before setting out on a journey, at seeing a comet, and when wearing new clothes. There are prayers for pastries, fruit, vegetables, and wine.[2] When I first learned of this tradition in seminary I was so charmed that I learned the *Ha-Motzi*, the blessing prayer for bread, the only one I can still say in Hebrew:

Baruch Atah, Adonai Elohenu, Melech Ha-Olam, Ha-Motzi Lehem Min Ha-Aretz.

"Blessed are You, Lord our God, King of the Universe, who brings forth bread from the earth."

As many different *brakoth* as there are, they all start out this same way: "Blessed are You, Lord our God, King of the Universe." Upon receiving good news, an observant Jew says, "Blessed are You, Lord our God, King of the Universe, who are good and beneficent." Upon receiving bad news, the *brakha* is "Blessed are You, Lord our God, King of the Universe, the Judge of Truth."

Because I am not a Jew, I try not to expound on what Jewish faith means. It is enough for me to try and act on my own faith, which has taken the tradition of blessing prayers under its wing. These blessings happen in church all the time. We bless bread, wine, water, oil, babies, couples, teachers, teenagers, elders, the sick, and the dearly departed. Episcopalians are fools for blessing things. We will even bless church furniture, embroidered kneeling cushions, religious jewelry, and silverware.

When I was a parish priest, I was often asked to officiate at the blessing of a home, which I did with pleasure since too many people thought holiness was reserved for God's house, not theirs. I did not take anything with me but a prayer book and a little brown vial of holy oil that I slipped into my pocket. The people who lived in the house supplied everything else from their own drawers and cupboards: the candles for the rooms, the cup and plate for communion, the bread, the water, and the wine. Some of them got so anxious ahead of time that they called to make sure they got the details right. What kind of wine should they buy? Was there a particular kind of bread? "The kind you eat," I said. "Same thing with the wine. Serve the kind you drink, and if you don't, Welch's grape juice will work just fine." They invited their friends, some of whom believed in God and some of whom did not. I could argue with myself on this, but I am not sure that you have to believe in God to pronounce a blessing. It may be enough to see the thing for what it is and pronounce it good. For most of us, that is as close to God as we will ever get anyway. To participate in a house blessing, all you have to do is to care about the people who live there. You constitute a blessing simply by showing up.

When everyone was accounted for, I began the service with a prayer, using the oil from my pocket to mark the lintel over the front door with the sign of the cross. If something bad had happened in the house, I said a prayer asking God to crowd the unclean spirits out. Then different people read bits of scripture, passing the Bible from hand to hand. Then someone who lived in the house lit a candle and we followed that person from room to room, lighting a candle in each one and saying prayers that blessed what happened in that room. In the kitchen, we blessed the hands that worked there, asking God to give us grateful hearts for daily bread. In the bedroom, we blessed hours of rest and refreshment for the people who slept there. In the workshop, we blessed the labor done there, that those who did it might share the joy of creation with God.

My favorite prayer was the one we said in the bathroom. Trying to get everyone in there was always tricky, as was finding a place for the candle. Nine times out of ten it ended up on the toilet tank, unless the bathroom was a fancy one with two basins and lots of counter space. Many things happen in a bathroom, as you know, and not all of them rise naturally to the lips in prayer. Private prayer, maybe, but not public, with a bunch of your friends and your priest all standing there fully clothed.

Not many people know it, but both Martin Luther and Julian of Norwich did some of their best thinking on the toilet. The blessing prayer for the bathroom strikes me as a perfect compromise between truth and tact.

O holy God, in the incarnation of your Son our Lord you made our flesh the instrument of your self-revelation: Give us a proper respect and reverence for our mortal bodies, keeping them clean and fair, whole and sound; that, glorifying you in them, we may confidently await our being clothed upon with spiritual bodies, when that which is mortal is transformed by life; through Jesus Christ our Lord. *Amen.*[3]

After we had blessed all the rooms we ended up in the living room again, gathering around the table our hosts had set for Holy Communion. After the bathroom prayer, this was my second favorite part. I loved seeing what people had decided to use on their home communion tables. We were all so used to the starched white linen at church that an old crocheted tablecloth looked wrong at first. Stained with spots from a dozen Thanksgivings, with the shadow of a round burn from a hot pan and not too expertly ironed, it looked too homely for a holy meal—but that, I think, was not the cloth's fault. It was our fault, for being so clumsy at blessing ordinary things, for failing even to look for the holiness in a wooden table, a stained tablecloth, a three-dollar loaf of bread.

Having just practiced this life skill in the kitchen and in the bathroom, we continued in the dining room. We looked at the table, set with the same kinds of dishes most of us ate on at home. We looked at one another's faces, gilded ever so slightly by the glow of the candles on the table. We blessed the ordinary bread and the ordinary wine, passing them between our ordinary hands to place in our ordinary mouths, and as we did so we were fed—by God, I should say, but also by one another. God has no hands but ours, no bread but the bread we bake, no prayers but the ones we make, whether we know what we are doing or not. When Christians speak of the mystery of the incarnation, this is what they mean: for reasons beyond anyone's understanding, God has decided to be made known in flesh. Matter matters to God. The most ordinary things are drenched in divine possibility. Pronouncing blessings upon them is the least we can do.

As I said earlier, the practice itself will teach you what you need to know. Start throwing blessings around and chances are you will start noticing all kinds of things you never noticed before. Did you ever notice the white and black striped stockings on the stick legs of that blessed mosquito before? Did you ever notice the tiny purple flowers on that blessed moss? One liability of pronouncing blessings out of doors is that it gets hard to walk on things. Once you become aware of the life in them, the kinship can really slow you down.

The same is true of other people. The next time you are at the airport, try blessing the people sitting at the departure gate with you. Every one of them is dealing with something significant. See that mother trying to contain her explosive two-year-old? See that pock-faced boy with the huge belly? Even if you cannot know for sure what is going on with them, you can still give a care. They are on their way somewhere, the same way you are. They are between places too, with no more certainty than you about what will happen at the other end. Pronounce a silent blessing and pay attention to what happens in the air between you and that other person, all those other people.

No one's spiritual practice is exactly like anyone else's. Life meets each of us where we need to be met, leading us to the doors with our names on them. Yet because we are human, we almost never go where no one has gone before. I remember once when I went on a walk through the woods near my house. It had rained the day before. The path under my feet was soft. The air was fragrant with damp bark and leaf rot. I was glorying in my aloneness when I came to a wash in the trail, where yesterday's rain had deposited a fresh layer of silt. Looking down, I saw that it was really a guest book, signed with deer hooves, turkey feet, snail trails, and three paws of a raccoon. I was hardly alone. I was in the middle of a parade, with life going ahead of me and more life coming along behind me to lay down its print next to mine.

THROUGH THE CENTURIES, people practiced at pronouncing blessings have come to some common wisdom, which they have laid down for the rest of us following along behind them. The first piece of wisdom is that a blessing does not confer holiness. The holiness is already there, embedded in the very givenness of the thing. The mosquito does not need your help to make it holy. The heavy boy at the airport does not need you to place him in divine custody, suggesting that perhaps while he is there he could lose a little weight. Because God made these beings, they share in God's own holiness, whether or not they meet your minimum requirements for a blessing.

This idea begs debate, especially in a culture sold on cosmetic surgery, home improvement, physical fitness, and the Protestant work ethic. Surely it makes more sense to withhold a blessing until something has become the best it can be? Surely there are some things that are so repulsive, worthless, or destructive that blessing them would be like aiding the opposition? The only way to find out is to try it. Practice blessing something simply because it exists alongside you and find out what your mind does with that exercise.

Find out what the judge inside you has to say about what you are doing. *Who gave you the right to call that dump blessed? Who do you think you are, anyway?* Find out how much humility is required, followed by how much mercy. *Where did you get the eyes to see the holiness in a dump like that? Who taught you to do that?* Notice what happens inside you as the blessing goes out of you, toward something that does not deserve it, that may even repel it. *If you can bless a stinking dump, surely someone can bless you.*

In Jewish tradition, every blessing prayer begins by blessing God.

"Blessed are you, Lord our God, King of the Universe, by whose word all things come into being."

"Blessed are you, Lord our God, King of the Universe, who has made the works of creation."

"Blessed are you, Lord our God, King of the Universe, who feeds all living things."

Such prayers are addressed to the God whose rain falls on the just and the unjust, whose sun rises on the evil and the good. In this complicated world, baby rattlesnakes get breakfast as well as baby girls and boys. Little Hitlers grow up in the same generation with little Bonhoeffers and little Schindlers. Blessing prayers do not overlook such complexity or the pain and suffering that can accompany it. They simply decline to adjudicate it. Rightly or not, they decide that given a choice between a blessing and a curse, a blessing will do more to improve air quality. A blessing will have more power to transform the blessee, although transformation is not required. There is no impressive logic behind this reasoning. The only logic is that all life comes from God, and for that reason alone we may call it blessed, leaving the rest to God.

A second piece of wisdom about pronouncing blessings, directly related to the first, is that the practice requires you to ease up on holding the line between what is bad for you and what is good. Once you get into the blessing business, you give up thinking you are smart enough always to tell the difference between the two. You surrender the fruit of the tree of the knowledge of good and evil (see the book of Genesis). You say a blessing when you break a bone the same as you do when you win the lottery. The two events may be more alike than you know. Live with either of them very long and you may discover that neither of them is as bad or as good as you first thought it would be. The blessing covers your ignorance and seeds your curiosity all at the same time. So this is what life has brought you! How will this change things? What can you make of this?

I have a friend who did not sleep through the night for years because of a dreadful dream he had. He did not have it every night, but he feared it every night, so that even on his nights off he stayed on guard. In the dream, a malevolent being showed up at the door of his house wanting something. As the monster banged on his door so hard that the wood bulged, he scrambled around the house looking for a weapon big enough to kill it, but every time he opened the door and killed it, the demon became larger. When he flailed at it, he said, some of the monster flew off and got on him. The part that got on him took him over, like a raging infection he could not stop. Killing the demon, he became part of it, so that he woke up with his wet sheets wound around him like bandages.

One night—*in the dream*—it occurred to him that what the demon wanted from him was his blessing. That was the only thing that would end the demon's agony. That was the only thing that would make it go away. So he opened the door with his guts on fire and his hands in front of his face.

"I bless you," he said to the demon, "and I bid you go where God wants you to go." But saying it once was not enough. He had to say it over and over again, as many different ways as he could think of to say it, for what seemed in the dream like close to an hour. It was as if the demon could not get enough of the blessing. It was as if no one had ever blessed him before.

"I bless you in the name of the Christ," my friend said for the hundredth time, "now go in peace." Making a sound like a kitten, the demon turned around and never came back.

This last piece of wisdom may be only for those who are very advanced at blessing prayers, but what most of them say is that pronouncing a blessing puts you as close to God as you can get. To learn to look with compassion on everything that is; to see past the terrifying demons outside to the bawling hearts within; to make the first move toward the other, however many times it takes to get close; to open your arms to what is instead of waiting until it is what it should be; to surrender the justice of your own cause for mercy; to surrender the priority of your own safety for love—this is to land at God's breast.

To pronounce a blessing on something is to see it from the divine perspective. To pronounce a blessing is to participate in God's own initiative. To pronounce a blessing is to share God's own audacity. This may be why blessing prayers make some people uncomfortable. As a loyal churchwoman once said in my hearing, "I don't want to be that important." Yet she relied on me, her priest, to say the blessings she was unwilling to say herself— because she knew they were necessary, because she needed to hear a human voice pronouncing God's blessing on her the same way she needed food and water, because otherwise she might give in to the insistent idea that she truly was not important, that both she and the whole world, including the people she loved, were without any significant meaning.

She counted on me to raise my hands in the air on a regular basis and ask God to bless her. She belonged to a whole congregation that was willing to pay people like me so that we would not be otherwise engaged when they needed one of us to lay hands on a baby, or a sick person, or a loaf of bread, or one of them. They did not need anyone to tell them that blessings confer meaning. They could feel it when a blessing landed on them, like warm oil poured on their crowns of their heads.

·   ·   ·

MY FATHER DIED after a small seizure caused by his advanced brain cancer knocked him for a loop two weeks before Christmas. After the seizure was over and the ambulance had taken him to the hospital, my mother and I followed in my car. Soon his small cubicle in the emergency room was full of my sisters, their sons, and our husbands, all crowded on a white bench set against the wall. The doctors and nurses checked my father's pupils, took his blood, rolled him over so they could replace his bathrobe with a hospital gown. They were in no hurry. No one spoke to my father, except one nurse who scolded him for wetting the stretcher.

Clearly, this was no emergency. These professionals had seen lots of old men die and this one was no different. Watching them do their work, the rest of us gradually realized that my father was dying too. Two weeks before Christmas, the hospital was full, or at least the floor where they put the people who were waiting to die. Because there was no room in the inn, the medical staff left us for long stretches. During these lulls, one or the other of us would get up and go to my father, standing over him so the harsh examining room light did not shine straight in his eyes. One of us would kiss him all over his forehead. Another would dip a pink sponge on a stick in water to wet his mouth. He was dazed from the seizure, but he knew who we were.

My mother and I lamented calling the ambulance. We should have kept him at home, we confessed to each other in low voices. But it *had* seemed an emergency to us. Watching him go rigid on the couch in the living room, we forgot that he was not ever going to get better. We did what we were taught to do when we were afraid someone was going to die. We called 911, forgetting that even they could not prevent him from dying. My sisters joined us with their own rehearsals of remorse, as the husbands and sons held our arms and rubbed our backs.

While we were doing this, I noticed my husband get up and go over to my father, leaning down to say something in his ear. They had long loved each other. Years earlier, they had gone on a canoe ride meticulously planned, outfitted, directed, and concluded on schedule by my sometimes maddeningly compulsive father. Everything had gone according to plan—my father's plan— throughout which Ed had been uncharacteristically compliant. Then right at the end, when they were almost safe on dry land, Ed tipped the canoe as he got out of it and dumped my father in the river.

"I hope that was an accident," Ed said when my father surfaced, his Cabela's outfit soaked through with the same green water he was spewing out of his mouth. That my father had laughed at this memory was a testament to his love for my husband, who in the present was kneeling down on the linoleum floor by my father's bed to fit his head underneath my father's bony hand. As I watched, Ed reached up and put one of his big hands on top of my father's hand to make sure it did not slip off. Then he held still while my father's lips moved. After he stood up, he leaned over to say something else in my father's ear.

"What was that?" I asked when he came back to slump beside me again.

"I asked him to bless me," Ed said. "I asked him to give me his blessing."

THIS KIND OF blessing prayer is called a benediction. It comes at the end of something, to send people on their way. All I am saying is that anyone can do this. Anyone can ask and anyone can bless, whether anyone has authorized you to do it or not. All I am saying is that the world needs you to do this, because there is a real shortage of people willing to kneel wherever they are and recognize the holiness holding its sometimes bony, often tender, always life-giving hand above their heads. That we are able to bless one another at all is evidence that we have been blessed, whether we can remember when or not. That we are willing to bless one another is miracle enough to stagger the very stars.

So I end where I began, at the wedding of spirit and flesh, practicing reverence with the living and the dead. I hope you can think of a dozen chapters I left out of this book. I hope you can think of at least that many more ways to celebrate your own priesthood, practiced at the altar of your own life. As the love poet of all time reminds us both,

> Today like every other day we wake up empty
> and frightened. Don't open the door to the study
> and begin reading. Take down a musical instrument.
> Let the beauty we love be what we do.
> There are hundreds of ways to kneel and kiss the ground.[4]

Acknowledgments

T he author wishes to thank both the Louisville Institute and Piedmont College for support during the writing of this book, portions of which have appeared in very different form in *The Christian Century, Home by Another Way* (Cowley, 1999), *Leaving Church: A Memoir of Faith* (HarperSanFrancisco, 2006), and *Explorations in Theology and Vocation*, edited by William E. Rogers (Furman University, 2005).

Thanks also to Stacie Burmeister for looking up arcane details on everything from the names of falling star showers to the makers of wooden clothespins, to Trisha Senterfitt for allowing me to cite her unpublished doctoral dissertation on walking the labyrinth, to Tommy and Collin Lines for sharing their labyrinth with me, to Curtis Bradford for reawakening me to the beauty of the French language, to Lisa Mahone for practicing the domestic arts with me, and to students at both Piedmont College and Columbia Theological Seminary for being my companions on the way.

Finally, I am grateful to Tom Grady for representing me with care and humor, and to the crew at HarperOne for seeing this work into print.

Notes

EPIGRAPH
1. Scott Cairn, *Love's Immensity: Mystics on the Endless Life* (Brewster, MA: Paraclete Press, 2007), 5–6.

CHAPTER 1: THE PRACTICE OF WAKING UP TO GOD
1. Genesis 28:16–17.
2. 2 Samuel 7:5–6.

CHAPTER 2: THE PRACTICE OF PAYING ATTENTION
1. Paul Woodruff, *Reverence: Renewing a Forgotten Virtue* (New York: Oxford University Press, 2001), 4.
2. Woodruff, *Reverence*, 46.
3. Diane Ackerman, *A Natural History of the Senses* (New York: Random House, 1990), 270.
4. Exodus 3:3.
5. Exodus 3:5.
6. Simone Weil, *Waiting for God*, tr. Emma Craufurd (New York: Harper & Row, 1951), 166.
7. Julian of Norwich, *Showings*, tr. Edmund Colledge, O. S. A., and James Walsh, S. J. (New York: Paulist Press, 1978), 342.

CHAPTER 3: THE PRACTICE OF WEARING SKIN
1. Cited by Dorothee Soelle in *The Silent Cry: Mysticism and Resistance* (Minneapolis: Fortress Press, 2001), 117.

2. Stanley Hauerwas, "The Sanctified Body," in *Embodied Holiness,* ed. Samuel M. Powell and Michael E. Lodahl (Downers Grove, IL: InterVarsity Press, 1999), 22.
3. Samuel M. Powell, "Introduction," op. cit., 9.
4. Powell, "Introduction," 194.

CHAPTER 4: THE PRACTICE OF WALKING ON THE EARTH
1. "The Labyrinth: Embodied Prayer and Healing," Trisha Lyons Senterfitt (unpublished Doctor of Ministry Project Report for Columbia Theological Seminary, 2006), 28–29.
2. Exodus 3:5.

CHAPTER 6: THE PRACTICE OF ENCOUNTERING OTHERS
1. *Lesser Feasts and Fasts* (New York: Church, 2003), 127.
2. Thomas Merton, *The Wisdom of the Desert* (New York: New Directions, 1970), 47. Merton is my source for the stories in this chapter; his small book contains the best introduction to the sayings of the Fathers that I know.
3. Merton, *Wisdom of the Desert,* 49.
4. Merton, *Wisdom of the Desert,* 54.
5. Merton, *Wisdom of the Desert,* 42.
6. Jonathan Sacks, *The Dignity of Difference* (New York: Continuum, 2002), 58.
7. Sacks, *Dignity of Difference,* 46.
8. Miroslav Volf, *Exclusion & Embrace* (Nashville: Abingdon Press, 1996), 20.
9. A phrase borrowed from John Courtenay Murray, as cited in *Religion in American Public Life,* ed. Martin Marty (New York: Norton, 2001), 129.
10. Jonathan Sacks, *The Dignity of Difference,* 60.
11. Merton, *Wisdom of the Desert,* 60.
12. Merton, *Wisdom of the Desert,* 59.

CHAPTER 7: THE PRACTICE OF LIVING WITH PURPOSE
1. Gustaf Wingren, *Luther on Vocation* (Philadelphia: Fortress Press, 1957), 72.
2. Cited by Matthew Fox in *The Reinvention of Work* (San Francisco: HarperOne, 1994), 14.
3. *The Song of God,* trans. Swami Prabhavananda and Christopher Isherwood (New York: Mentor, 1972), 40.

CHAPTER 8: THE PRACTICE OF SAYING NO
1. Abraham Heschel, *The Sabbath* (Boston: Shambhala, 2003), 3.

2. Alexis de Tocqueville, *Democracy in America,* rev. ed., vol. 2 (New York: The Colonial Press, 1899), 355.

3. Craig Harline, *Sundays: A History of the First Day from Babylonia to the Superbowl* (New York: Doubleday, 2007).

4. Mollie Ziegler Hemingway, "The Decline of the Sabbath," *The Wall Street Journal,* June 15, 2007.

5. Matthew 6:26–29.

6. *Gates of Prayer,* ed. Chaim Stern (New York: Central Conference of American Rabbis, 1975), 245.

7. Judith Shulevitz, "Bring Back the Sabbath," *New York Times,* March 2, 2003.

CHAPTER 10: THE PRACTICE OF FEELING PAIN
1. For a fascinating study by someone who is, see Ariel Glucklich's *Sacred Pain: Hurting the Body for the Sake of the Soul* (New York: Oxford University Press, 2001). Glucklich's insights guided my own throughout the writing of this chapter.

2. Job 7:19.

3. Job 6:4.

4. Job 9:17.

5. Job 16:12.

6. Job 16:13.

7. Job 30:30.

8. "Love Dogs," *The Essential Rumi,* tr. Coleman Barks with John Moyne (San Francisco: HarperOne, 1995), 155.

9. Job 13:13–15.

10. Job 38:2.

11. Job 40:2.

12. Job 40:4–5.

13. Job 42:5–6.

14. Barks, *The Essential Rumi,* 152.

CHAPTER 11: THE PRACTICE OF BEING PRESENT TO GOD
1. Robert Bly, *The Kabir Book* (Beacon Press, 1977), as quoted in *gratefulness, the heart of prayer* (New York: Paulist Press, 1984), 7.

2. Brother Lawrence, *The Practice of the Presence of God,* tr. Robert J. Edmonson, ed. Hal M. Helms (Orleans, MA: Paraclete Press, 1985), 109.

3. Brother Lawrence, *The Practice of the Presence of God,* 91.

4. Brother Lawrence, *The Practice of the Presence of God,* 94–95.

5. *Gratefulness,* 22.

CHAPTER 12: THE PRACTICE OF PRONOUNCING
BLESSINGS
1. Wendell Berry, *A Timbered Choir* (Washington, DC: Counterpoint, 1998), 134.
2. Rabbi Joseph Telushkin, *Jewish Literacy* (New York: Willima Morrow, 1991/2001), 736–738.
3. *The Book of Occasional Services,* 2nd ed. (New York: The Church Hymnal Corporation, 1988), 147.
4. *The Essential Rumi,* tr. Coleman Barks with John Moyne (San Francisco: HarperOne, 1995), 36.

Permissions